Praise for *Divided We Fall*

"*World* magazine's 'Understanding America Book of the Year.' The U.S. is more polarized than at any time since the Civil War. The highly discussed book that best recognizes that—and proposes what to do—is David French's *Divided We Fall*." —*World* magazine

"[French is] not calling on us to agree—just to continue disagreeing without destroying ourselves." —Carlos Lozada, *The Washington Post*

"[French] offers a timeless reminder of the importance of justice, mercy, and humility toward one another— imperfect people in an imperfect world, still hoping for a more perfect union." —Terri Barnes, *Stars and Stripes*

"French presents a vision for how the country can come together again and embrace national unity." —Mackenzie Dawson, *New York Post*

"French laments conspiracy-minded rhetoric from both the right and the left in this incisive examination of contemporary political polarization. This well-informed and often moving account provides an antidote to the ills of political partisanship." —*Publishers Weekly*

DIVIDED WE FALL

America's Secession Threat
and How to Restore Our Nation

DAVID FRENCH

ST. MARTIN'S GRIFFIN
NEW YORK

Published in the United States by St. Martin's Griffin,
an imprint of St. Martin's Publishing Group

www.stmartins.com

Designed by Steven Seighman

The Library of Congress has cataloged the hardcover edition
as follows:

Names: French, David, 1969– author.
Title: Divided we fall : America's secession threat and how to restore
our nation / David French.
Description: First edition. | New York : St. Martin's Press, 2020. |
Includes bibliographical references and index. |
Identifiers: LCCN 2020016432 | ISBN 9781250201973 (hardcover) |
ISBN 9781250201980 (ebook)
Subjects: LCSH: Political culture—United States. | Polarization
(Social sciences)—Political aspects—United States. |
Secession—United States. | Culture conflict—United States. |
Identity politics—United States. | Social media—Political
aspects—United States. | United States—Politics and
government—21st century.
Classification: LCC JK1726 .F667 2020 | DDC 306.20973—dc23
LC record available at https://lccn.loc.gov/2020016432

ISBN 978-1-250-83673-1 (trade paperback)

Our books may be purchased in bulk for promotional, educational,
or business use. Please contact your local bookseller or the
Macmillan Corporate and Premium Sales Department at
1-800-221-7945, extension 5442, or by email at
MacmillanSpecialMarkets@macmillan.com.

First St. Martin's Griffin Edition: 2022

10 9 8 7 6 5 4 3 2 1

*To Nancy. You turn ordeals into adventures
and fill our family with joy.*

*To James Madison. May we remember
that you were right.*

CONTENTS

INTRODUCTION: A House Divided   1

PART I: THE RELENTLESS MOMENTUM OF OUR MUTUAL CONTEMPT

1. Understanding the Geography of American Division   31
2. Geography Plus Culture Plus Fear Equals Secession   40
3. The Kindling Awaits the Spark of Fear   49
4. America Cannot Repeat Even Its Recent History of Violence 56
5. How an Academic Paper Explains America   63
6. Churches and Cities, the Core of Group Polarization   71
7. Politics Trumps Everything   81
8. From Extreme to Mainstream, Time and Again   86
9. The Shifting Window of Acceptable Discourse   93
10. Losing the Free Speech Culture   101
11. Losing a Common Political Language   110

PART II: THE DISSOLUTION

12. Calexit   119
13. Texit   144
14. A World on Fire   165

PART III: TO SAVE AMERICA, CHART JAMES MADISON'S COURSE

15. Pluralism, a Beginner's Guide   177
16. Rediscover Tolerance   185

17. Can Anyone Pass the Tolerance Test?   196
18. Can Moments of Grace Make a Movement of Grace?   202
19. To Go Forward, We Must Go Back   210
20. Immigration Breaks the Federalist Will   217
21. Could California Health Care Reform Revive
      American Federalism?   223
22. Federalism Ends Where the Bill of Rights Begins   229

    CONCLUSION: A Call for Courage   241

ACKNOWLEDGMENTS   259
NOTES   261
INDEX   269

How is it possible for there to exist over time a just and stable society of free and equal citizens, who remain profoundly divided by reasonable religious, philosophical, and moral doctrines?

—JOHN RAWLS

A House Divided

It's time for Americans to wake up to a fundamental reality: the continued unity of the United States of America cannot be guaranteed. At this moment in history, there is not a single important cultural, religious, political, or social force that is pulling Americans together more than it is pushing us apart. We cannot assume that a continent-sized, multi-ethnic, multi-faith democracy can remain united forever, and it will not remain united if our political class cannot and will not adapt to an increasingly diverse and divided American public.

We lack a common popular culture. Depending on where we live and what we believe, we watch different kinds of television, we listen to different kinds of music, and we often even watch different sports.

We increasingly live separate from each other. The number of Americans who live in so-called landslide counties—counties where one presidential candidate wins by at least twenty points—is at an all-time high. The geography that a person calls their home, whether it be rural, exurban, suburban, or urban, is increasingly predictive of voting habits.

We increasingly believe different things. America is secularizing at a rapid rate, but it is still the most religious nation in the developed world, and is set to remain so for the indefinite future. While the "religious nones" (those with no particular religious affiliation) grow in number, many of America's most religiously fervent denominations are growing as well, some rapidly. Moreover, America's secular and religious citizens are increasingly concentrated in different parts of the country, supplementing geographic separation with religious separation.

We increasingly loathe our political opponents. The United States is in the grip of a phenomenon called "negative polarization." In plain English this means that a person belongs to their political party not so much because they like their own party but because they hate and fear the other side. Republicans don't embrace Republican policies so much as they despise Democrats and Democratic policies. Democrats don't embrace Democratic policies as much as they vote to defend themselves from Republicans. At this point, huge majorities actively dislike their political opponents and significant minorities see them as possessing subhuman characteristics.

Moreover, each of these realities is set to get worse. Absent unforeseen developments, the present trends are self-reinforcing. Clustering is feeding extremism, extremism is feeding anger, and anger is feeding fear. The class of Americans who care the most about politics is, perversely enough, the class of Americans most likely to make negative misjudgments about their fellow citizens. Our political and cultural leaders are leading us apart.

Given this reality, why should we presume that our nation is immune from the same cultural and historical forces that have caused disunion in this nation before and in other nations countless times?

I'm writing this book from a unique position. For the first time in my life, I'm a man without a party. I have no "tribe." And I must confess that it has opened my eyes. I see things differently than I used to, and I understand the perspective of my political opponents better than I did before.

For a long time you didn't have to convince me of the problems with the American left. As a Christian conservative lawyer, I dedicated much of my professional life to protecting free speech and religious freedom. I've been a pro-life activist my entire adult life. In 1992, I formed a pro-life student group at Harvard Law School, and I've been writing, speaking, fundraising, and litigating to protect unborn children ever since.

I filed my first constitutional case more than twenty years ago. I represented my local church in a dispute with our local zoning board and was grateful to win a victory that launched a litigation career that took me into federal courts from coast to coast. But I wasn't just a civil liberties lawyer; I was a proud Republican. I bought the whole package—or what I thought was the package.

Ronald Reagan was the first president I truly followed, and to my young mind he wasn't just right on the issues, he inspired me. He appealed to my highest ideals. He asked us to be our best selves. No, I didn't think he was perfect—even my young teen self could see that he was human, and like all humans, he had profound flaws. No politician is perfect. But between Reagan and the first President Bush, a brave and decent man who led by example, I believed I understood the leadership model for the Republican Party. The GOP didn't just share my political values, it shared my moral values. It was the party of good (but imperfect) people *and* good (but imperfect) ideas.

In the 1990s, I believed the distinctions between Republican and Democrat sharpened. I had seen the Democrats more charitably, as people of good character but flawed ideas. Then I watched, utterly appalled, as the Democrats circled the wagons around Bill Clinton. He was a liar. He was an adulterer. Women came forward to accuse him of sexual misconduct so severe that Democrats would have demanded that any Republican facing such accusations resign. There was even strong evidence that he was guilty of rape—yet there he was, basking in the roar of the Democratic crowds, behaving like a rock star at the 2000 Democratic National Convention, even after the sordid details of the worst claims against him had been aired all over national television.

Yes, I could see that multiple Republicans faced their own sex scandals. Newt Gingrich was having his own affair even as Republicans pursued Clinton, for example. But I possessed the normal partisan mind. The normal partisan is able to see flaws on his own side—only a fanatic is totally blind to their side's faults—but he sees them as exceptional. Flaws on the other side, by contrast, are emblematic. They're a "tell," providing evidence of the underlying ideological or moral rot of your opponents.

When confronted by wrongdoing in his own tribe, the normal partisan indignantly turns to the media and to their fellow citizens and demands, "Don't judge us by the crazy few." And then, just as indignantly, he looks at the worst actors from across the aisle and says, "Look at what your ideas cause. Look at what they're *really* like. The mask has slipped."

Moreover, partisans know their own narratives inti-
mately. We believe our own stories. And my story was
that I was a son of the New South—the region that had
turned the page on its racist past. Yes, voting was still
divided between black and white, but *this time* the white
vote was about the Cold War, about faith, and about economics. The race wars were over, the culture war was
under way, and it was only a matter of time before our
Christian African American brothers and sisters recognized that reality and began to separate from their secular, progressive allies.

It's not that I believed my opponents were evil. In
fact, I zealously defended the civil liberties of my political opponents. I believed then (and still believe) that
the blessings of liberty accrue to all Americans, and the
rights of my political opponents are every bit as precious
as the rights of my political allies. Yet nothing truly shook
my deep conviction that the GOP was just better. It was
the party of better people and better ideas. It was the
party of my friends and neighbors, and my friends and
neighbors were people I loved and often admired.

My political opponents, by contrast, I saw as increasingly angry—increasingly unhinged at the extremes—
and dangerous for the long-term health of the republic. I
believed that even when my progressive friends were ster-
ling individuals in their personal and professional lives,
their political ideas were deeply misguided, and their bad
ideas were leading to bad outcomes for America.

By the middle of the second George W. Bush administration, I was so deeply entrenched in partisanship
that shortly before I deployed to Iraq (I was then a cap-
tain in the Army Reserve) in 2007, I gave a speech at

a conservative conference where I actually made this ridiculous statement: "I believe the two greatest threats to America are university leftism at home and jihadism abroad, and I feel called to fight both."

Then I went to war. And now I'm ashamed of those words.

It's one thing to understand intellectually William Tecumseh Sherman's observation that "war is hell." It's another thing entirely to see it up close. Let me be clear: I served as a JAG officer (Army lawyer) for an armored cavalry regiment. I am not in any way comparing my service to the cavalry scouts and armor officers who went outside the wire every day, facing IEDs, mortars, and snipers. But I lost friends. I felt the tension of driving across uncleared roads deep into enemy-held territory. I know what it's like to patrol through hostile towns and villages.

And I saw what one human being can do to another. The atrocities were horrifying. I watched a DVD that was left in the dust of an empty village, a DVD featuring al Qaeda terrorists beheading innocent women and cheering like they'd scored a soccer goal even as they sawed off their heads. We received a report of a man who placed a bomb in his unwitting nephew's backpack and remotely detonated it at his own brother's wedding. In one awful incident, a terrorist shot a three-month-old baby to death in front of its mother, then shot the mother as she cradled her son's body in her arms.

Our area of operations was known for a time as the female suicide bombing capital of the world. Terrorists would "recruit" young women to transform themselves into bombs by raping them, thus "shaming" them (in their perverted worldview) so profoundly that only by martyring themselves could they receive redemption.

As I interacted with Iraqi police officers, soldiers, and translators, there were two things I noticed about the hatred that was then dominating Iraqi life. First, each side had its own *substantially true* narrative of grievance and atrocity. For every single example of Shiite violence, one could muster up a story of Sunni viciousness. And while it was absolutely correct that Saddam Hussein had brutally repressed the Shiite population, by 2007 the Shiite militias had made it abundantly clear that they could give as good as they got.

Second, the conflict itself thus became reason enough for sustaining the conflict. While the combatants may have had some sense of the ultimate policy differences in a Sunni- or Shiite-dominated Iraq, as a general rule the motive for the fight was much more primal—those horrible people cannot be permitted to win. The person who killed a brother, son, mother, or uncle had to die. It's trite to say "violence begets violence," but it's quite often simply true. When a militia slaughters a family member, it's human to seek vengeance. Across the scope of human history it's *normal* to seek vengeance. The aberration is the modern embrace of the rule of law and the shedding of revenge for justice.

But in spite of the rage and violence, by September 2008, we believed we'd prevailed. After years of blood-soaked civil war and counterinsurgency, al Qaeda in Iraq seemed to be a broken, spent force. We routed it from our area of operations, and I watched with my own eyes as the province seemed to stir back to life. Markets returned. Villages repopulated.

What was one sign of our success? When we'd arrived in November 2007, we'd flown into our base, as al Qaeda largely controlled the roads, and driving risked unacceptable losses. In late September 2008, when my unit left, it drove out, confident that it could cross the province unmolested. In November 2007, any given mission had faced a 25 percent chance of enemy contact. That meant a one-in-four chance of an IED strike, sniper attack, ambush, or mortar barrage. By the next September—after months of hard, costly fighting—the chances of an attack had dropped to as low as 1 percent.

I landed back in the United States later that month in a nation that seemed to be moving in the opposite direction from Iraq. The Iraqi nation seemed to be reviving. America was sliding toward an economic disaster. Lehman Brothers had filed for bankruptcy just a few short days before, the stock market was in chaos, and an angry public was so weary of war that most Americans didn't seem to know or care that we'd turned the tide.

Then, on one of the first days back at my civilian job (I worked as a senior counsel for a Christian public interest law firm), one of my colleagues—a young rising star in Christian conservative ranks—invited me to join an "urgent conference call." He described it as a call that could "change the course of history."

I'm no fan of conference calls, but with that billing, how could I refuse? So, at the appointed time, I joined the call and learned its purpose—to discuss filing litigation that was supposed to ultimately prove that Barack Obama was a Kenyan and (likely) a Muslim and not constitutionally qualified to be president of the United States. I hung up the phone.

That call was jolting. I knew several people on the line. I had never before thought of them as our "crazies"—the weirdos who populate the fringes of every movement. Yet in my daily life I just kept meeting more people like them—respectable individuals from all walks of professional life who were convinced that Obama wasn't truly American. For years, I mocked the 9/11 "truthers," the (mostly) Democratic cohort who believed "Bush knew" about the attack on the World Trade Center, the people who believed 9/11 was an "inside job."

Suddenly I found myself around the Obama "birthers," and I kept trying to convince myself that they were an irrelevant fringe, that they did not reflect the true nature of the conservative movement. After all, their most prominent public advocate was Donald Trump, and he was a reality television star. Who listened to him?

My time in Iraq had changed me. It had also educated me. It changed my regard for my fellow citizens, especially my political opponents. If I had been willing to die for them while wearing the uniform of my country, why should I regard them as mortal enemies today? Wrong on the law and on policy, yes. But a threat to the country in the way I'd framed them before I went to war? No. Absolutely not. It was my responsibility to prioritize their liberty, prosperity, and human flourishing every bit as much as I prioritized those virtues for members of my own political tribe.

But I found myself woefully out of step with the times. My partisan polarization was decreasing just as years of cultural, religious, and geographic separation began to bear their bitter fruit. By 2016, the Republican Party I'd grown up in was barely recognizable to me. The party I perceived to be a party of hope had clearly become a party of rage. Concern about the course of American law, politics, and culture had become alarm, and alarm in some quarters turned to panic.

I heard the same comments time and time again: "If Hillary wins, America is over." Or "If Hillary wins, America is a socialist country." Or "If Hillary wins, we'll lose the Constitution." In September 2016, a man named Michael Anton wrote one of the most influential essays in modern politics. It was influential not because it was intellectually or morally sound but because it captured (and, crucially, rationalized) the spirit of the moment.

Called "The Flight 93 Election," it appeared in the prestigious *Claremont Review of Books*. It began memorably: "2016 is the Flight 93 election: charge the cockpit or you die." For Anton, the situation was so dire that you could figuratively charge the cockpit and still die—the country was so far gone that Trump might not be able to save it—but, in Anton's words, "a Hillary Clinton presidency is Russian Roulette with a semi-auto. With Trump, at least you can spin the cylinder and take your chances."[1]

Against the background of an emergency that grave, failure to join with Trump wasn't just a betrayal of the party, it was a betrayal of the nation itself. The people who opposed Trump were hurting America, and if those people were Republican or conservative, then they weren't just wrong like Democrats are wrong—they were traitors to the cause. They were stabbing the GOP in the back. The name Benedict Arnold re-entered American discourse.

But I knew that mindset already. I had seen it inflicted on my friends. I had seen it inflicted on my family. Beginning in 2015, when I began publicly critiquing Trump and his allies, my family was targeted by the so-called alt-right, online white nationalists who were fierce Trump supporters.

My youngest daughter is black, adopted from Ethiopia, and the alt-right took pictures of her seven-year-old face and Photoshopped her into a gas chamber, with Trump Photoshopped in an SS uniform, pushing the button to kill her. Her face was Photoshopped into old images of slaves working the fields of the Old South. My wife was accused of having sex with "black bucks" while I was deployed to Iraq, and I was called a "cuck," a racialized term that refers to a type of pornography in which a white man watches a black man have sex with his white wife.

Hundreds of horrifying messages filled my Twitter feed, but the harassment didn't stay on Twitter. Alt-right trolls found my wife's blog and filled the comments section with images of dead and dying African Americans. She was threatened via email, and in one bizarre moment a person hacked into a phone call with her elderly father and began screaming profanities at her and berating her about Donald Trump.

This was a small slice of a massive online onslaught against Trump critics. My friend Ben Shapiro was targeted with an avalanche of vile anti-Semitic attacks. By the end of the campaign, virtually any conservative Trump critic with any kind of meaningful platform could tell stories of racist, anti-Semitic, or other profane attacks.

And while the alt-right was fringe, the wider Republican public accepted and sometimes even cheered behavior that was beyond the pale. Whether responding to Trump's proposed Muslim ban, the *Access Hollywood* tape that recorded Trump bragging that he grabbed women by the genitals, Trump's extraordinary attacks on Mexican immigrants, Trump's praise of Vladimir Putin, or the women who came forward—often with corroborating evidence—accusing Trump of sexual harassment or sexual assault, there was a constant rationalization: support Trump, even with all his flaws, to save our nation.

By the midpoint of the Trump presidency, left and right were locked in a culture war so intense that even basic virtues like civility and decency were scorned. On the left, radicals mocked civility as "respectability politics." On the right, Trump apologists declared that in the face of the present emergency, decency was a "secondary" value. And like a (thankfully) milder version of the two sides of the Iraq War, both sides could recount a litany of moral atrocities, from actual acts of violence to online outrages and political perfidy.

The two competing narratives began to take clear shape. The left looks at the GOP and offers a critique that flows from the racial conflicts and racial divisiveness of the worst days in American history. From this perspective, a shrinking white Christian population, steeped in historical privilege, is lashing out as America becomes more racially and religiously diverse. The very man who most denied the legitimacy of the nation's first black president now leads a coalition of voters that is at best indifferent to racial justice and at worst outright racist. His own explicitly racist comments only seem to anchor his support in an angry white community.

In this narrative, these same voters are granted out-sized power by the quirks of America's white-supremacy-stained constitutional past. Thanks to the Electoral College and the Senate, an angry minority governs from the White House. An angry minority has a hammerlock on the Senate. In states across the nation, they use temporary majorities to try to engineer permanent control through gerrymandering and voter suppression. Thus, even if a majority of Americans demand change, they cannot obtain it, and as the GOP opposition to Merrick Garland demonstrated, not even a clean and clear presidential victory could guarantee the president's Supreme Court nominee so much as a hearing.

Even worse, continues the left's narrative, the angry white minority is inflicting cruelty as policy. How could a party that fashions itself as pro-life and pro-family endorse policies that led to mandatory family separation at the border? How could they look at themselves in the mirror as agents of the state ripped children from their mothers' arms?

Right-wing intolerance breeds cruelty, and it also breeds violence. Anger at necessary social change is spilling over into outright racism, homophobia, and Islamophobia online and in political rhetoric. And in some cases angry men are taking their rage into the real world, massacring worshippers in South Carolina and Pittsburgh, gunning down Latinos in an El Paso Walmart, committing a terror attack in Charlottesville, and inflicting violent hate on racial, religious, and sexual minorities in communities from coast to coast.

Compounding it all, the left's argument continues, the angry right elected an angry man, and then stubbornly defended him even as he was caught, time and again, in overt lies and obvious abuses of power. The same party that once impeached a man for lying about sex locked arms to defend a man who orchestrated a criminal scheme to pay hush money to a porn star, ran a political campaign that eagerly sought help from a hostile foreign power, and then—once in office—tried to force a desperate and dependent ally, the vulnerable nation of Ukraine, to engage in a politically motivated investigation of one of the president's chief domestic political opponents.

If you see these facts, the narrative concludes, how can you not be alarmed? Isn't it necessary to view your political opponents as dangerous? Isn't it foolish to believe they mean well?

The right has a competing narrative, one rooted in faith, history, and the nature of the American founding. It begins simply: They hate us, they lie about us, and they use all the instruments of their power to deprive us of our rights and even to deprive us of our jobs and economic opportunities. The left's message is clear—conform or lose your livelihood.

Even worse, in the name of social justice and so-called reproductive freedom, they have legalized killing on a mass scale. In the years since the unelected Supreme Court read a right to abortion into a Constitution that's utterly silent about the topic, tens of millions of innocent children have died in the womb. And leftists are fanatics about "the right to choose," resisting even the most modest attempts to restrict the deadly practice and even sometimes using their economic power to sanction states that resist.

According to the right's narrative, the left tramples individual liberty. In the name of "tolerance," they restrict free speech. In the name of "justice," they limit due process. In the name of "peace," they seek to limit the fundamental human and constitutional right of self-defense.

They will use any means necessary to accomplish their goals. If they have a social media account, they'll shame and humiliate you online. If they own a company, they'll impose economic punishments on states, cities, and towns—even as they're happy to do business with truly oppressive regimes like China or Saudi Arabia. If they run a university, they'll openly discriminate against conservative and Christian students and faculty. They'll harass people in restaurants. They'll harass people at movie theaters. They'll harass people at home.

Leftist anger breeds violence, continues this narrative. Remember the flames in Ferguson, Baltimore, and Charlotte? Remember the police officers ambushed in Dallas and Baton Rouge? Did you see antifa beating journalists? And who can forget the angry leftist who almost changed history with his attempted massacre of Republican congressmen on a Virginia baseball field?

And now they disrespect the constitutional order. They abused the counterintelligence surveillance powers to obtain a warrant against a former campaign aide, they used a fake dossier full of Russian disinformation to spread conspiracy theories and undermine public trust in the president, and then they rushed to impeach that same president for—at worst—a minor diplomatic mistake, one that was ultimately corrected before any harm was done. Oh, and they rushed to impeach after years before locking arms to defend a Democratic president after he was caught red-handed committing the federal crime of perjury and the federal crime of obstruction of justice. If it weren't for double standards, they'd have no standards at all.

If you see these facts, the right's narrative concludes, how can you not be alarmed? Isn't it necessary to view your political opponents as dangerous? Isn't it foolish to believe they mean well?

Note that each narrative is supported by a number of actual facts (mixed with distortions and exaggerations). Partisans are describing things that actually occur, are actually terrible, and cause real fear and harm. Black and Jewish Americans have been massacred in houses of worship. A left-wing political terrorist did try to assassinate GOP members of Congress. And the lesser violations have happened as well. The question, however, isn't whether these things occurred but rather whether they represent a true expression (or logical outcome) of your political and cultural opponents' motives, character, and actions.

At the core of each narrative is the burning conviction that the other side doesn't just want its opponents to lose political races, but rather wishes for them to exist in a state of permanent, dangerous (perhaps even deadly) subordination. And, really, if you're steeped in your own side's narrative, shouldn't your opponent not just lose but also be cast down from American politics and culture? Why should you tolerate such hate? Why should you respect their institutions and their autonomy?

One does not respect evil. One defeats evil. Justice requires nothing less.

The point of this book is not to adjudicate the competing narratives of left and right. Indeed, the effort is both futile and counterproductive. This book is not intended as yet another sledgehammer for right to use against left or left to use against right. The point of this book is to help the reader to understand these competing narratives and to warn against the product of their inexorable and relentless spread through the American body politic.

I grew up in rural America, I've lived in the heart of Trump country. I've lived in America's bluest precincts. I'm no longer a Republican. I'm not a Democrat. And I'm in neither tribe in large part because I feel that I understand both, and I believe both tribes can and must rediscover a sense of shared community and shared citizenship. But I don't think it's inevitable that they will. Simply put, we now face a renewed threat to our national unity. We're stumbling into the very state of being that James Madison addressed in Federalist No. 10: the "violence of faction."

To understand how to go forward, we must go back—to the wisdom of the Founders, men who knew that factions could tear America apart and conceived (at least in theory) of a solution that must resonate today.

A faction, Madison argued, is a "number of citizens" who are "united and actuated by some common impulse of passion, or of interest, adverse to the rights of other citizens, or to the permanent and aggregate interests of the community." Each side of our current divide would look at that definition and emphatically identify their opponents as adverse to their rights and to their communities.

Each side looks at the other and sees a threat that transcends normal political difficulties. While we still fight over conventional policy differences, the threat feels greater. The narrative of conflict transcends economic growth rates and gross domestic product. It transcends welfare policy or trade policy. The narrative of conflict is grounded in exactly the identities that have split nations and destroyed empires—race, religion, and ethnicity. It's grounded in tribalism.

And how does the body politic deal with a faction? By either removing its causes or controlling its effects. Removing its causes is perilous. According to Madison, one could remove its causes either "by destroying the liberty which is essential to its existence" or by "giving to every citizen the same opinions, the same passions, and the same interests."

The first remedy is oppressive, "worse than the disease," in Madison's words. "Liberty is to faction what air is to fire," he says, "an aliment without which it instantly expires." The observation that free speech gives life to and spreads hateful thoughts is the argument for a speech code. Extinguish the hateful speech, and you'll extinguish the hate. But Madison understands that extinguishing liberty has costs: "It could not be less folly to abolish liberty, which is essential to political life, because it nourishes faction, than it would be to wish the annihilation of air, which is essential to animal life, because it imparts to fire its destructive agency."

The second remedy, uniformity, is impossible. As

Madison observed, "As long as the reason of man continues fallible, and he is at liberty to exercise it, different opinions will be formed." In fact, the "latent causes of faction" are "sown into the nature of man."

How then does a functioning nation manage the challenge of faction? Madison has the answer—pluralism. A broad diversity of interests and groups across a federal union helps prevent any one interest or group from attaining dangerous dominance. In his words, "The increased variety of parties comprised within the Union, increase this security." He writes, "The influence of factious leaders may kindle a flame within their particular States, but will be unable to spread a general conflagration through the other States. A religious sect may degenerate into a political faction in a part of the Confederacy; but the variety of sects dispersed over the entire face of it must secure the national councils against any danger from that source."

In other words, the faction still enjoys liberty. It can still "kindle a flame." But the very existence of a robust republic consisting of different, competing communities and sects acts as an antibody against oppression. Thus, one of the core projects of a healthy American constitutional republic is to protect not just individual liberty, but the federalism and freedom of voluntary association that allow a multiplicity of groups and communities to flourish.

That's the great genius inherent in James Madison's crowning glory, the Bill of Rights. And the jewel in that crown is one of the greatest single sentences in the history of the English language, the First Amendment. It reads: "Congress shall make no law respecting an establishment of religion, or prohibiting the free exercise thereof;

or abridging the freedom of speech, or of the press; or the right of the people peaceably to assemble, and to petition the government for a redress of grievances."

We tend to think of the First Amendment as primarily protecting individual liberty, but it's a mistake to underestimate its vital role in protecting the right of association, the right to form groups and communities that reflect and advance your fundamental values. And it's this right of voluntary association that is the lifeblood of true pluralism. Its message to Americans of all races, religions, creeds, and sexual orientations is clear: Not only do you have a place in this society, it is a place secured even against the oppression of hostile majorities. You *and your community* can thrive in this American republic.

It's fashionable in modern times to emphasize the homogeneity of the Founders and the founding American states. Landowning white Christians governed the colonies, led the Revolution, and wrote the Constitution. Yet this modern view dramatically underestimates the true diversity of the founding. Think of the eastern seaboard of the new nation. Running from north to south were colonies that represented the profound religious differences of the new nation. There were puritans in Massachusetts, religious dissenters in Rhode Island, Quakers in Pennsylvania, Catholics in Maryland, and Anglicans in Virginia.

The very existence of these different communities was evidence of the fractiousness of the western Christian world. Many were the descendants of religious refugees from Europe. Rhode Island was founded by Roger Williams, a victim of religious intolerance in Massachusetts. The different sects represented many of the combatants in the Wars of Religion, arguably the most devastating conflicts on the European continent before the modern world wars.

The First Amendment's twin religious freedom guarantees—the guarantee of free exercise of religion and the guarantee of freedom from an established church—worked together to protect the theology, values, and autonomy of distinct religious communities. The preservation of those guarantees within the Constitution, immune from repeal in the absence of extraordinary political supermajorities, gave minorities a degree of protection from the push and pull of politics. No matter the outcome of an election, the rights and liberties of greatest import remained intact, and thus so could minority communities.

Moving beyond religion, the First Amendment also protects civil society itself, the formation of groups and associations that have traditionally provided Americans with a profound level of meaning and purpose. Alexis de Tocqueville's famous passage in *Democracy in America* is worth remembering:

> Americans of all ages, all conditions, all minds constantly unite. Not only do they have commercial and industrial associations in which all take part, but they also have a thousand other kinds: religious, moral, grave, futile, very general and very particular, immense and very small; Americans use associations to give fêtes, to found seminaries, to build inns, to raise churches, to distribute books, to send missionaries to the antipodes; in this manner they create hospitals, prisons, schools. Finally, if it is a question

of bringing to light a truth or developing a sentiment with the support of a great example, they associate. Everywhere that, at the head of a new undertaking, you see the government in France and a great lord in England, count on it that you will perceive an association in the United States.

Note the contrast. In the United States, the people form associations—associations protected by the supreme law of the land. The energy comes from the bottom up. In England and France, it came from the top down.

Make no mistake, the ideals of the American founding far outstripped the reality of American life. Madison, one of the fathers of American pluralism and the author of the Bill of Rights, owned slaves. Thomas Jefferson, the author of the Declaration of Independence—the man who wrote the words, "We hold these truths to be self-evident, that all men are created equal, that they are endowed by their Creator with certain unalienable Rights, that among these are Life, Liberty and the pursuit of Happiness"—owned slaves.

Slavery was our nation's original sin, though it was hardly our only sin. But we also know that the Founders and the founding documents created the inherent tension between America's ideals and America's sins, and we've seen Madison's pluralism bear fruit. When the variety of parties increases—when more voices are heard—the power of the most dangerous faction (or of any faction) decreases. Consider the sheer number of additional communities who've powered their way into American pluralism, so often by noting and amplifying the contrasts between America's ideals and America's sins.

The tide is turning, however. American civil society is retreating, and as American civil society retreats, politics surges to take its place. Healthy pluralism, whereby citizens find meaning in their communities and civic associations secure in the knowledge that the body politic will ultimately protect their autonomy, is in decline. It's being replaced by an increasingly bitter factionalism. The civic energy identified by de Tocqueville is fading, and the reliance on the government or the "great lord" (in this case, the president specifically or the federal government more broadly) is increasing.

To say this is not to break new ground. In books such as Robert Putnam's *Bowling Alone*, Charles Murray's *Coming Apart*, Jonah Goldberg's *Suicide of the West*, and Timothy Carney's *Alienated America*, one can trace the reality, causes, and consequences of American polarization and division. The purpose of this book isn't to repeat those arguments. It's instead to sound a different alarm. America was built from the ground up to function as a pluralistic republic. It can flourish only as a pluralistic republic. And, contrary to the beliefs of illiberal activists and intellectuals on the left and the right, America can exist only as a liberal, pluralistic republic. By "liberal," I do not mean Democratic or progressive but rather the form of government that "conceive[s] humans as rights-bearing individuals who could fashion and pursue for themselves their own version of the good life." According to liberalism, "opportunities for liberty [are] best afforded by a limited government devoted to 'securing rights,' along with a free-market economic system that [gives] space for individual initiative and ambition."[2]

And make no mistake, liberalism itself is under attack.

Even basic values like decency are under attack. In the summer of 2019, I found myself in the eye of an unusual online storm in the conservative world. The op-ed editor for the *New York Post*, Sohrab Ahmari, published an essay in *First Things* magazine called "Against David French–ism."[3] The essay went viral, triggering months of debate in virtually every conservative publication in America.

Ahmari made three broad arguments. First, politics was rapidly devolving to a state of "war and enmity." Second, in such circumstances, civility and decency were "second-order values." Indeed, in some circumstances they may be undesirable. And third, liberalism itself was responsible for perceived declines in American culture. Why was I a part of this equation? Because in my support for both civility and the liberal order (in particular, my support for civil liberties), I was inadequate for the challenge of the times. The path of "David French–ism" was allegedly retreat and defeat. Ahmari's goal, by contrast, was to "fight the culture war with the aim of defeating the enemy and enjoying the spoils in the form of a public square re-ordered to the common good and ultimately the Highest Good."

To put things more bluntly, I recognize pluralism as a permanent fact of American life and seek to foster a political culture that protects the autonomy and dignity of competing American ideological and religious communities. Ahmari and many of his allies on the right seek to sweep past pluralism to create (and impose) a new political and moral order, one designed according to their specific moral values—and to the extent that individual liberty conflicts with the "common good" or "Highest Good," it must be swept away.

That's a vision for domination, not accommodation. It's a vision directly contrary to the spirit of Federalist No. 10, and it's a vision that's ultimately unattainable. Indeed, as I'll explain in the pages that follow, the quest for moral, cultural, and political domination by either side of our national divide risks splitting the nation in two (or in three or four).

This book is divided into three parts. In Part I, I describe in detail how the combination of geographic sorting, group polarization, and individual intolerance isn't just dividing Americans individually and collectively, it's dividing Americans in the ways that are most dangerous for continued national unity. Our competing red and blue regions are geographically contiguous and culturally distinct. They're also economically powerful and increasingly hostile to their political competitors.

They're also, contrary to the Madisonian vision, decreasingly autonomous and less able to chart an independent course. Just as the nation has grown more ethnically and religiously diverse and features an increasingly complex technology-driven economy that caters to individual choice to a degree that capitalists of the past could scarcely imagine, our government has grown more centralized, less democratic, and increasingly focused around one person—the president—who functionally possesses executive, legislative, and judicial power to a degree that would shock the drafters of the U.S. Constitution.

Americans are by now tired of being told that each and every presidential election is somehow "the most important election of our lifetimes," but as the legal and practical power of the president continues to grow, each and every presidential election elects the most powerful peacetime leader in American history. It gives the leader of one faction inordinate, unintended influence and control over all other American factions. Madison's pluralistic safeguards do not hold, and an increasing number of Americans then view the president as an actual enemy, a person of awesome power who is actively trying to strip them of their liberty and dignity.

Talk of civil strife is in the air. On the right, populist writers are penning popular fictions about a second American civil war. Serious thinkers on the left and the right produce essays advocating various strategies for winning a "cold civil war." This language sounds hysterical—especially to everyday Americans who pay little attention to politics—but it is heartfelt, and it's amplified in the American political class in part because those who are angriest, those who are most panicked, often tend to be the citizens most likely to be engaged in politics.

In Part II of this book, I'll attempt to answer the incredulous critics who can't *imagine* a new American secession. I'll chart out two scenarios for American dissolution, one based in California, the other in the South. Each of these regions is carving out its own distinct culture and straining at current legal and political limits to dissent from national political mandates. The scenarios I describe will be based on presently discussed and presently debated statutes and proposed legal changes. They imagine what will happen if a critical mass of Americans believe their liberty or safety are irrevocably in the hands of people they perceive as hating them and despising their way of life.

It's time for our warring tribes to understand a simple reality: that to embrace illiberalism and intolerance is to court dissolution. At the extremes, it even risks civil war. As I said at the start of this chapter, there is not a single important cultural, religious, political, or social force that is pulling Americans together more than it is pushing us apart.

In Part III, I discuss the solution. To go forward, we have to go back—to the principles of Federalist No. 10. Our nation should be a nation that sustains and nurtures "an increased variety of parties." It should protect a legal system and culture that in turn protect a "variety of sects dispersed over the entire face" of continental union.

That does not mean for a moment that any citizen abandons their faith, their truth claims, or their quest to end injustice as they see it. It does mean, however, that this quest is to be accomplished—whenever possible—through persuasion and minimal necessary coercion. It means restraint in imposing unwanted systems on unwilling communities unless essential civil liberties are at stake. It means changing a narrative that is presently teaching each great American faction that every national political loss is a reason for existential despair. And perhaps most importantly, it requires an act of common citizenship—extending yourself to fight for the rights of others that you would like to exercise yourself.

To protect pluralism isn't to surrender hope for change. As Frederick Douglass wrote in 1860, free speech is the "great moral renovator of society and government." Free speech, "of all rights, is the dread of tyrants. It is the right which they first of all strike down. They know its power."[4] Nor does the defense of pluralism abandon government as an instrument for the common good. Instead it channels that quest within bounds of necessary restraint, with deep respect for dissent.

But to embrace pluralism is to surrender the dream of domination. To embrace pluralism is to acknowledge that even the quest for domination is dangerous. It understands that human beings will not yield that which is most precious to them, even at the point of a gun. Embracing pluralism means embracing the lessons of history and understanding that not even our great nation is immune to the forces that have fractured unions older than ours. Our nation's angriest culture warriors need to know the cost of their conflict. As they seek to crush their political and cultural enemies, they may destroy the nation they seek to rule.

PART I

The Relentless Momentum of Our Mutual Contempt

Understanding the Geography of American Division

In the first six months of 2019, the United States experienced an unprecedented, geographically concentrated wave of legislation directly aimed at the single most contentious public controversy in the country. First the state of Ohio and then the states of Kentucky, Tennessee, Georgia, Alabama, Mississippi, Louisiana, and Missouri all passed bills that either banned abortion outright, banned it after a fetal heartbeat can be detected, or banned it if the Supreme Court overturned *Roe v. Wade*.

The bills were mostly passed by legislative supermajorities, and the end result was to create an immense geographic region—populated by more than 52 million Americans—that intends to be almost entirely abortion-free.

At the same time, competing abortion bills were proposed and passed in multiple northern states. Most notably, New York and Illinois passed laws that liberalized abortion rights up to the moment of labor and delivery. By the end of 2019, contrasting American abortion laws began to roughly mirror the North/South divide at the start of the Civil War. Once more, and for a very different reason, the South was becoming a land apart.

Any discussion of American division has to start with geography. American diversity isn't uniform in the fifty states. Not all states are equally religious, they're not equally racially diverse, and they're not remotely culturally equivalent. Increasingly, red and blue Americans live in separate locations, enjoy separate media, and hold separate religious beliefs.

We're all familiar with the red and blue American maps. Most Americans live in a state that's either solidly Republican or solidly Democratic, and it's not just the states that are unified around a single political party. Consider the growth of the so-called landslide county, a county that one party or the other wins by at least twenty points. In 1992 only 38 percent of American voters lived in a landslide county. In 2016 that number hit a record 60 percent.[1]

In a nation less sharply divided by party *and* region, one would expect a blue-surge election like 2018's to yield a number of state legislatures moving from solid red (with the upper and lower chambers both Republican) to divided, with one chamber red and the other blue. Instead, even in a blue surge, only one state legislature flipped from united to divided. Instead, the blue wave resulted in greater consolidation. In blue states, divided legislatures united under Democratic control. In other words, by the end of Election Day, the states were more politically uniform, not less.

Consequently, as of 2019 there was exactly one state with divided legislative control—Minnesota. The legislatures of the other forty-nine states are controlled by a single party. Republicans control thirty-one state legislatures, and Democrats control eighteen.

But what about the "trifectas," those states where the same party controls both chambers of the legislature and the governor's mansion? Before the 2018 election, the trifecta states were at near-record highs. A total of thirty-four states were under trifecta control, twenty-six Republican and eight Democratic.

After the election? The number of trifecta states grew. Now thirty-seven states are under trifecta control, twenty-three Republican and fourteen Democratic.

And these states aren't checkerboarded across the country. Instead, red and blue states tend to be geographically clustered. Democrats have lockdown control of the Pacific Coast. The states of Washington, Oregon, and California are progressive strongholds. Democrats also have extensive control of greater New England—an area they'd almost completely dominate but for the success of moderate Republican governors in Massachusetts and Maryland, states that nonetheless remain thoroughly Democratic and progressive.

The Republicans persistently dominate the states of the Southeastern Conference (yes, the center of American college football power is also the center of Republican political and cultural dominance), but they also dominate large sections of the American West and Upper Midwest.

For the politics-obsessed, this division is alarming (or enraging) enough. It signals that each party faces a geographic wall of opposition, and political dissenters sometimes feel as if they're trapped behind (ideological) enemy lines. But the political division is merely the tip of the iceberg. Our geographic divisions are cultural and religious as well, and these deeper divisions reinforce and amplify the political divide.

This trend reflects the "big sort," a term coined by Bill Bishop in his 2008 book by the same name. Americans "have been self-segregating by lifestyle, though not necessarily politics, for several decades," and now their votes are beginning to reflect their different lifestyles. As Bishop notes, "We're sorting by the way we live, think and—it turns out—every four years or every two years, how we vote."[2]

In fact, one can overlay the electoral map with any number of additional maps, including church attendance maps or even maps of television ratings, and see clearly the stark cultural divides. A map of church attendance is strikingly similar to a map of voting habits. According to Gallup data, each of the states with the lowest church attendance votes Democratic. Each of the states with the highest and above-average attendance votes solidly Republican. Most of the states with below-average attendance are blue.[3]

Keep in mind that for tens of millions of believers, church attendance is a cultural marker that reflects the most profound and important beliefs in their lives. A Christian or secular identity is as important to Americans as a Sunni or Shiite identity is to Iraqis or a Muslim or Hindu identity is to Indians. The actual church-attending American is typically not a mere casual believer.

Church isn't a social club. Religious faith isn't a political ideology. It's a statement of belief about nothing less important than eternity itself. So when you review the geography of faith, you're seeing the extent to which our states (and entire regions) are populated by people with fundamentally different beliefs about life, death, sin, and redemption.

Moreover, these political and religious divisions are enduring. We have reached a remarkable degree of self-sustaining stasis in core red and blue America. Let's pick up after the 1988 election, the last true Electoral College blowout in American politics. From that point forward, the citizens of the Northeast, the Southeast, and the Pacific Coast have built red and blue walls so high and formidable that true swing states simply don't exist within their geographic cores.

The Pacific Coast is a deep blue political and cultural enclave. California last went Republican in 1988. Oregon and Washington last went Republican in 1984. Since 1988 those three states have created a coherent blue culture on the West Coast.

California is now the heart of Democratic political, economic, and cultural power in the United States. In 2018 the state possessed the fifth-largest economy in the world—larger than Britain's and only smaller than those of Germany, Japan, China, and the rest of the United States. Add Washington and Oregon to the mix, and this three-state western nation would challenge Germany for the world's fourth-largest economy.[4]

Now let's move south. Or, more precisely, let's move to the South and the Upper Midwest. The unchallenged red wall encompasses all of the states of the NCAA's Southeastern Conference (excluding swing state Florida)—that's Texas plus Missouri, Kentucky, Tennessee, South Carolina, Georgia, Alabama, Mississippi, Arkansas, and Louisiana. But it also includes a vast unbroken region located north and west of Texas. Democrats haven't won the states of Oklahoma, Kansas, Nebraska, South Dakota, North Dakota, Wyoming, Idaho, and Utah since *1964.*

This conglomeration of states represents yet another immense economic entity. Combine those economies—rich with natural resources—and they would quickly rival Japan for the third-largest economy in the world.

We can't neglect the Northeast. The line of states running up the eastern seaboard from Maryland represents yet another blue wall and yet another culturally distinct economic powerhouse, representing the fourth-largest economy in the world. Indeed, it's a symbol of the sheer size and power of the American economy that you could break off these three sections of America, and they would immediately represent three of the top ten world economies—and that's without allocating any swing states to any new American nation.

Moreover, the red and blue political distinctions in these regions are just one symptom of the large cultural gap. As just noted, the red wall includes every single state with the highest church attendance rate (with the exception of North Carolina) and the vast majority of the states with the highest rates of gun ownership.[5] The blue wall represents secular America, and the coasts are among the most lightly armed segments of American society.

When Barack Obama spoke of the section of America that clings to "God and guns," he was speaking of this immense red wall. When progressive Americans speak of the arc of history, they dream of transforming the rest of the nation into New York, California, or Massachusetts.

Moreover, much the way Virginia played a central role in the Confederacy, as its most populous and powerful state, each of these geographic regions contains a key state, a cornerstone economic and cultural power: California in the West, Texas in the South, and New York in the Northeast.

So that's politics and religion. What about pop culture? Aren't we at least bound together by common interests? No, we are not. The staggering multiplicity of entertainment choices prevents any single television show or pop artist from dominating the national conversation, but it's also true that interests are not spread evenly across the United States. Instead, different shows are popular in different regions and with different cultures.

In late 2016, the *New York Times* published a series of ratings maps that showed exactly how a show can be popular without breaking through cultural and ideological lines.[6] Take one of my favorite shows, the late, lamented *Game of Thrones*. The *Game of Thrones* map is the Hillary map. Its appeal is heavily clustered in deep blue coastal cities, something that's completely unsurprising to this suburban Tennessee resident. Around here I have a hard time finding anyone who watched the show, much less someone who cares enough to do a deep dive into Westerosi lore.

Do you reject *Game of Thrones*, George R. R. Martin's epic series? Then your television drama is more likely to center around the Grimes gang in the AMC hit *The Walking Dead*, the entertainment industry's valentine to the Second Amendment.

Geographic differences are even obvious when you look at American sports. The NBA is largely an urban sport, pulling its fans from America's deep blue cities. Those fans don't mind the politicization of its athletes.

They cheer its "woke" stars. College football is a far more rural and exurban sport, and its fans have little patience for politics and plenty of enthusiasm for ostentatious pre-game patriotic displays.

The NFL is different. It's arguably the last major American sport that truly reaches across all political lines and depends on its universal appeal for its ratings and financial dominance. If it pulled in NBA or college football ratings numbers, it would collapse. It's built to be America's pastime.[7]

But the NFL now divides as much as it unites. Until the New England Patriots' come-from-behind miracle Super Bowl win over the Atlanta Falcons, the single biggest story of the 2016 NFL season was political—Colin Kaepernick's decision to take a knee rather than stand respectfully for the national anthem. Overnight, one of America's last "safe spaces" from politics became yet another ideological battle space.

The battle only intensified when Donald Trump intervened. After Trump called for kneeling players to be fired at a 2017 rally in Florida, hundreds of players kneeled. The president had challenged them directly, and men who had built their careers and identities around their toughness and courage were not going to be intimidated.

And so, for weeks on end, Sunday afternoon didn't represent a respite from politics, it was the epicenter of a culture war surrounding questions of free speech and patriotism. As we watched football games, we weren't just raging at an ill-timed blitz or lamenting a dropped pass; we were asking what it meant to be American.

Put all these trends together, and you can see the

vast and growing political and cultural gap in the United States, centered around American geography.

In fact, multiple researchers are tracking this phenomenon and registering its political and cultural effects. Leading publications publish story after story documenting our geographic divisions. Consider these headlines from the data-driven website FiveThirtyEight:[8]

> *"Purple America has all but disappeared."*
> *"The polarization of red and blue states, from*
> *McGovern to Trump, in one chart."*
> *"Migration isn't turning red states blue."*
> *"The House and Senate are the most divided they've*
> *been in our lifetimes."*
> *"As swing districts dwindle, can a divided House*
> *stand?"*

The collective message is clear. Religious, political, and cultural divisions have manifested themselves in an emerging, divided American geography, and history teaches us that—under certain specific circumstances—divided geography can sow the seeds of disunion.

Geography Plus Culture Plus Fear Equals Secession

In the 134 years since the Army of Northern Virginia surrendered to the Army of the Potomac at Appomattox, there have been few more intense historical and political battles than the battle over the causes of the Civil War. In many ways, that battle is over, and the Lost Cause myth that minimized the role of slavery in secession has blessedly lost.

To be crystal clear, I do not intend to refight any aspect of that conflict. I'm not here to advance the Lost Cause myth, to glorify the Confederacy, or to excuse any aspect of secession. As every reasonable person knows, the single most important cause of secession and the resulting Civil War was slavery. The South did not secede for "states' rights." It did not secede as part of a virtuous quest for self-determination. No, it seceded to preserve (and potentially even spread) the singularly evil institution of race-based slavery.

If you have the slightest doubt about any of this, just read what the secessionists wrote and said when they separated from the Union. From Alexander Stephens's infamous "Cornerstone" speech to the declarations of secession by the various states—their own versions of a declaration of independence—they laid out with great clarity the reasons for their decisions to break the nation.[1] Absent the dispute over slavery, the South would not have seceded, and absent the moral gravity over the vile reason for secession, one wonders if the Union would have had the will to continue the brutal, bloody fight that followed.

But the focus on slavery can obscure other aspects of secession—the aspects I'm going to focus on now. We know the fundamental reason the South seceded, but the *timing* for secession—and the stated justifications— need to be examined in greater detail. As every American student is taught, the first African slaves arrived at the Jamestown colony in 1619—which was 242 years before secession. So by 1861, the American colonies and the American nation had experienced centuries of slavery. Yes, it was contentious. Yes, it was divisive. But it was also the norm.

To put this immense time period in perspective, the Thirteenth Amendment—which abolished slavery—was ratified on December 6, 1865. We will have to live on this continent more than eighty additional years before the time after slavery will match in length the time during slavery. And if you include the century of Jim Crow that existed before the passage of the Civil Rights Acts in 1964, formal legal subjugation of African Americans endured for a stunning 345 years.

Throughout early American history, politicians reached multiple compromises that balanced slave and free political power, preventing the growing North from gaining decisive control (especially in the Senate), but nothing could stop North and South from growing apart; nothing could stop the creation and cultivation of two different cultures in two different sections of the country. And nothing was stopping the North from growing in population and power.

While the arc of history was trending toward industrialism and the expansion of a free society built on the labor of free individuals, this national transformation was not uniform. It was not penetrating a vast region of the United States. Thus, to that region, northern power appeared entirely hostile. It wasn't just an opposing political power, it was an opposing culture. It was an opposing economic model. It presented an alternative way of life that was incompatible with and economically superior to the South's slave society.

By the election of 1860, the South possessed all of these characteristics:

1. It was large and geographically contiguous—it possessed the mass and economy of a significant nation-state.
2. It was relatively culturally homogenous— possessing a common language, a common faith, and a distinct way of life (centered around its slave culture and the slave economy).
3. It believed that its culture and essential liberties were under threat (the perceived threat of northern anti-slavery factions led southerners to believe slavery faced inevitable decline).
4. It was consumed with an unreasonable fear of violence and a belief that white northern radicals actively wanted to harm the people of the South.

The first three elements made white southerners believe that secession was a viable, perhaps even necessary, counter to growing northern power. The last element, however, is often overlooked in contemporary discussions of the Civil War. The last element made many southerners believe that secession was an urgent, immediate imperative. Modern Americans who so rightly revile slavery glide past the fact that not every effort to defeat slavery was peaceful. We forget the blood that was spilled in the years before the Civil War.

In fact, some of slavery's most famous opponents were vicious, murderous men, and their actions put fear in the hearts of southerners from Virginia to Texas. Those fears were stoked and inflamed by secessionist politicians and secessionist media to the point that there were men and women who supported secession partly as an act of self-defense—as the only way to guarantee the physical safety of their families. In other words, the underlying conditions for secession existed for some time, but it took an extra shove to make it happen.

One of those shoves—arguably the biggest shove—was the election of Abraham Lincoln in 1860. But he came to the White House against the backdrop of pervasive fear.

It's long been understood that white southerners lived in fear of a slave rebellion. (It's an odd aspect of Old South culture that many southerners argued that slaves were happier and more content than northern factory laborers but at the same time feared that those allegedly happy and content slaves would revolt and kill them in their sleep.) It's less commonly understood how that fear of slave rebellion played an arguably critical role in secession.

Take, for example, Nat Turner—the man who led the 1831 slave revolt in Virginia that was most recently depicted in the Nate Parker film *The Birth of a Nation.* Portrayed as a hero in the movie, Turner was in reality a brutal mass murderer. When Turner launched his real-life revolt, it wasn't so much a battle against white oppression as it was a pure killing spree—a mass murder of fifty-seven people that included women and young children. Turner's men hacked kids to death.[2] In one instance, they attacked a school. In another, they reportedly returned to a house after they realized they'd left a child alive. They killed an infant in its cradle and dumped the body in a fireplace.[3]

After the militia put down the rebellion, numerous white citizens responded with an even worse killing spree of their own, lynching perhaps more than two hundred black men and women, slave and free. As more militia poured into the region (rumors of a more widespread rebellion were swamping the South), they committed unspeakable atrocities—torturing, burning, and decapitating suspected slave insurgents, often without the slightest pretext or evidence.[4]

Ultimately, Virginia authorities intervened to stop the terror, but the killing then moved to the courts, where seventeen more men were sentenced to death. Across the South, the revolt triggered a wave of fear, anguish, and hate. Some called for the end of slavery, others for the expulsion of slaves, and still others threatened to exterminate the black population.[5]

The psychological effect was profound. Innocent black men and women suffered vicious violence. Calls for emancipation fell largely on deaf ears, and the response to the rebellion mainly served to tighten the slavers' grip. Hundreds of thousands of white southerners lived in terror of another revolt, and when John Brown tried in 1859 to launch a mass-scale slave rebellion by seizing the federal arsenal at Harpers Ferry, many interpreted it as attempted mass murder.

After Brown's capture and execution, northern abolitionists celebrated him and treated him as a righteous martyr in a holy cause; white southerners believed that northern radicals wanted them dead.

In his seminal one-volume history of the Civil War, *Battle Cry of Freedom*, James McPherson describes the contrasting southern and northern responses to Brown. At first northerners approached Brown with a sense of "baffled reproach," but by the end of his trial, leading northern figures like Theodore Parker and Ralph Waldo Emerson praised Brown to the heavens. Parker wrote that Brown was "not only a martyr . . . but also a SAINT." Emerson said that Brown would "make the gallows as glorious as the cross."[6]

McPherson paints a vivid picture of northern reverence for Brown:

> Extraordinary events took place in many northern communities on the day of Brown's execution. Church bells tolled; minute guns fired solemn salutes; ministers preached sermons of commemoration; thousands bowed in silent reverence for the martyr of liberty. "I have seen nothing like it," wrote Charles Eliot Norton of Harvard. More than a thousand miles away in Lawrence, Kansas, the editor of the *Republican* wrote that "the death of no man in America has

ever produced so profound a sensation. A feeling of deep and sorrowful indignation seems to possess the masses." A clergyman in Roxbury, Massachusetts, declared that Brown had made the word Treason "holy in the American language"; young William Dean Howells said that "Brown has become an idea, a thousand times purer and better and loftier than the Republican idea"; Henry David Thoreau pronounced Brown a "crucified hero."[7]

As McPherson notes, most of Brown's eulogists drew a contrast between his "errors of judgment" and the "nobleness of his aims"—even to the point of calling his raid on Harpers Ferry "insane." Horace Greeley called it "the work of a madman."

But this "distinction between act and motive was lost on southern whites." They were cast into an "unreasoning fury." They perceived "only that millions of Yankees seemed to approve of a murderer who had tried to set the slaves at their throats." The resulting public reaction to northern approval of Brown "provoked a paroxysm of anger more intense than the original reaction to the raid."

Again, here's McPherson:

The North "has sanctioned and applauded theft, murder, treason," cried *De Bow's Review*. Could the South afford any longer "to live under a government, the majority of whose subjects or citizens regard John Brown as a martyr and a Christian hero?" asked a Baltimore newspaper. No! echoed from every corner of the South.[8]

Indeed, if one looks at the formal declarations of secession, the fear that the North was intent on inciting a slave revolt is repeated time and again. And when white southerners thought of an insurrection they thought of Nat Turner, of children being hacked to death in their homes.

For example, the state of Georgia's lengthy official declaration of secession—in addition to its long defense of slavery—alleged that "for twenty years past the abolitionists and their allies in the Northern States have been engaged in constant efforts to subvert our institutions and to excite insurrection and servile war among us."[9]

Georgia's secession declaration is hardly unique. Mississippi's much shorter declaration of secession specifically references northern support for John Brown and condemns abolitionists who "invested with the honors of martyrdom the wretch whose purpose was to apply flames to our dwellings, and the weapons of destruction to our lives."[10] South Carolina's declaration specifically accuses the North of attempting to "disturb the peace" and incite "servile insurrection."[11]

Texas went even further, accusing abolitionists of seeking to *poison* innocent Texans, claiming they had "sent hired emissaries among us to burn our towns and distribute arms and poison to our slaves for the same purpose."[12]

To be clear, the southern fear that the northern states wanted to see mass white killings in the South was unreasonable. Yes, there were radicals, like John Brown and some abolitionist allies, who wanted to see a mass slave rebellion and knew that mass death would result. Yet in 1860 abolitionism was hardly dominant in the

North, and Abraham Lincoln made it as clear as he could that he had no intention of abolishing slavery.

Southern states weren't wrong to discern the irresistible political, economic, and cultural momentum of the free states, but to actually fracture the country, the secessionists needed something else. They had to create a sense of emergency. Secession required a very real fear. And it required a belief that powerful citizens in the North actually hated the citizens of the South—hated them enough to want them dead.

When those feelings are isolated into small communities—or perhaps sprinkled throughout a larger country—even fear and rage won't result in secession. There just isn't sufficient cultural, economic, or political mass to form a new nation. In 1861, however, the South perceived itself to be strong. It had "King Cotton," it had immense territory, it had a cohesive culture, and it had a population of fighting men that it believed could form a mighty army.

In fact, many of these elements of secession were present in the American founding, the secession that launched our new nation. A distinct culture housed in a geographically distinct region feared the loss of its liberty, and it believed that its opponents exhibited disregard for their very lives. By 1775, American culture had grown distinct from the mother country, the colonists feared the loss of their essential liberties, and the presence of British troops dramatically escalated the stakes of political confrontation. The conditions were ripe for revolt.

The Kindling Awaits the Spark of Fear

So, let's talk about today. Where do we stand on the crucial four factors that helped create American secession? As we've discussed, the rock-solid enclaves of red and blue America are both geographically contiguous and—in many ways—culturally distinct. When we say "red" and "blue," we mean more than politics. We often mean a way of life.

Of course, that's not to say that the American union is presently precarious or that there is presently any serious secession movement, but it is true that two of the essential preconditions for national divorce exist. There are geographically contiguous, culturally distinct regions of the United States that have long maintained those distinctions and are set to maintain those distinctions for the foreseeable future.

But what about the next condition? Do the populations of these regions believe that their culture and their essential liberties are under threat? The answer here is unquestionably yes. It is now increasingly clear that virtually every major American political difference represents and reflects an aspect of the series of American culture wars.

Even court decisions and laws that work small changes in citizens' everyday lives take on immense importance not just because of the underlying principles animating the conflict, but also because of the identities of the combatants. Each small legal loss is deemed but the first step on the road to repression.

Behind the red wall sits an enormous percentage of America's most religious citizens, and for these citizens the loss of religious liberty is perceived not just as a threat to their way of life but also as a statement of hatred and contempt from their fellow citizens. In fact, the loss of religious liberty has historically been a casus belli for innumerable conflicts. Religion matters, and current legal arguments are paving the way for a near future in which all too many American citizens must choose between obedience to government and obedience to the eternal dictates of their faith.

Putting aside for a moment the constitutional merits of the argument for gay marriage, there were many millions of Christians who saw the Supreme Court's decision in *Obergefell v. Hodges* as an ominous sign that their "first freedom" was in peril. In one sense, it's an odd concern. *In theory* the legalization of gay marriage should have little to do with religious liberty. After all, surely a nation that has room for competing faiths can also have room for competing visions of marriage, right? Not so fast—not when the expanded regulatory state seeks not just to change the law but also to change the culture. Never forget these actual words from President Obama's solicitor general during oral arguments in *Obergefell*:

Justice Samuel Alito: Well, in the Bob Jones case, the Court held that a college was not entitled to tax-exempt status if it opposed interracial marriage or interracial dating. So would the same apply to a university or a college if it opposed same-sex marriage?

Solicitor General Donald Verrilli: You know, I—I don't think I can answer that question without knowing more specifics, but it's certainly going to be an issue. I don't deny that. I don't deny that, Justice Alito. It is—it is going to be an issue.

Just after the 2016 presidential election, law professor David Bernstein highlighted that exchange and called the *Obergefell* argument the "oral argument that cost Democrats the presidency."[1] While there are many things that cost Democrats the presidency, that moment is certainly one of them. Think for a moment of the cultural and legal implications.

Culturally, this is the president's lawyer casting traditional Christians outside the boundaries of mainstream American society, placing them in the same category as racists for upholding a biblical definition of marriage. Legally, he's raising the possibility that the schools and institutions educating young Christian kids by the millions could face the choice between compromising their values and financial crisis, or even institutional extinction.

And keep in mind that this statement occurred in the context of a generation-long campaign of elite demonization of Evangelical Christian belief and practice. In my own law practice, I witnessed more than a hundred colleges and universities attempt to bar one or more Christian student groups from campus—mainly on the grounds that it was "discriminatory" for Christian groups to reserve leadership positions for Christian students. I represented Christian students who were told they had to change their religious beliefs to earn degrees from public universities.

Moreover, the solicitor general made his statement mere weeks after Christians watched aghast as our nation's largest and most powerful corporations gang-tackled the state of Indiana for having the audacity to enact its own Religious Freedom Restoration Act, which did little more than reinstate traditional legal protections for religious liberty. This corporate attack was supplemented by an absurd media pile-on as reporters on the hunt for anti-gay bigotry fixed their eyes on a previously unknown pizza store simply because it *hypothetically* wouldn't serve pizza at a gay wedding.

Think of the magnitude of the First Amendment concerns in the minds and hearts of Americans behind that red wall. How *dare* a central government dictate to me how I raise my children? How *dare* reporters hunt for Christian business owners for the purpose of ridicule and reprisal?

In my conversations with progressives, they consistently underestimate the seismic cultural impact of progressive corporate decisions to sanction states that protect religious liberty or pass pro-life laws.

What progressives see as conventional activism for a righteous cause, conservatives perceive as punitive economic sanctions and expressions of hatred. In fact, given that multiple major corporations threaten to sanction red

states like Georgia, Indiana, Alabama, and North Carolina while eagerly doing business in truly oppressive regimes in China and Saudi Arabia, the perception is that
progressives despise their fellow citizens more than they
dislike actual tyrants. In other words, it's not just the
sanctions that so alarm conservatives, it's the perceived
loathing behind the sanctions.

The NBA, for example, moved its all-star game from
Charlotte, North Carolina, after the state passed its so-
called bathroom bill, a law that required individuals in
public buildings to use bathrooms that corresponded with
the gender listed on their birth certificate. By contrast,
in late 2019, numerous NBA players and officials apolo-
gized to China and the Chinese people when the general
manager of the Houston Rockets, Daryl Morey, tweeted,
"Fight for Freedom, Stand with Hong Kong" (and then
quickly deleted the tweet).

Again, the perception is that major American cultural
institutions are angrier at their mainstream domestic
political opponents than they are at actual hostile and
oppressive foreign governments.

Of course, thus far I've focused on the legal and cultural concerns of citizens behind the red wall. But what
about the legal and cultural concerns in blue America?
Here it's also clear that blue citizens see red governments
as threats to their essential freedoms.

Take, for example, the Trump administration's attack
on California's sanctuary cities and on the state's comprehensive statutory scheme designed to protect illegal
immigrants from federal law enforcement by limiting the
extent to which California officials are permitted to cooperate with federal immigration authorities. On March

6, 2018, the Trump administration filed a comprehensive federal lawsuit against California, seeking to invalidate its sanctuary state laws.[2]

To many millions of California citizens, the Trump administration's action decisively demonstrated its hostility against undocumented Latino immigrants. How so? Because the administration was willing to cast aside long-held Republican ideas about America's constitutional structure in its quest to ramp up deportations.

Under basic principles of federalism, there is nothing legally wrong with California's laws. The federal government, as a general rule, may not "commandeer" state officials to enforce federal law, and (so long as they do not actively hinder the work of federal authorities) state officials may allocate state resources according to state priorities.

California's laws protecting illegal immigrants, establishing "sanctuary cities," and keeping state officials out of federal immigration enforcement reflect "California values"—the desires of California's citizens to be welcoming to otherwise law-abiding immigrants regardless of their legal status. That is a debatable policy decision, and it has profound economic and cultural effects, but it is *California's decision to make.*

But not according to the Republican Trump administration. The administration has filed a lawsuit to override and actively force state officials to violate state policies, to contradict "California values," in a manner that brings actual suffering to men, women, and children living in the state.

And that's but one issue. There are citizens living behind the blue wall who have—in large numbers—exactly the opposite views regarding, for example, religious liberty and gun rights than do citizens behind the red wall. They perceive the proliferation of guns in private hands as a threat to the health and welfare of their communities. They believe that the enforcement of religious liberty laws (especially when applied to schools and businesses) closes off opportunities to LGBT citizens and brings back the terrible memory of Jim Crow.

Moreover, principles and values that many red Americans perceive to be nothing more than "political correctness" reflect—in the minds and hearts of many millions of progressives—a serious effort at cultural reform designed to correct the effects of deep and grievous historical injustices.

Again, the purpose of this book is not to debate the merits of these positions, but to acknowledge and accurately describe the immense depth of feeling surrounding them, along with the depth of anger when a distant central government (especially if it's working through an unelected Supreme Court) overrides the self-governance of either red or blue communities. Red and blue fear is real. Rage is growing. Thankfully, fear and rage have not yet triggered widespread violence. I'm not certain that the American body politic could absorb even the violence of the recent past.

America Cannot Repeat Even Its Recent History of Violence

So if citizens of these geographically contiguous, culturally distinct regions feel as if their way of life and fundamental liberties are under threat, then why isn't the nation *already* facing imminent threat of division?

I'd submit it's because the fourth condition— unreasonable fear—has not yet been met. There is obviously no occupying force in American cities like the redcoats in Boston, and, thankfully, there is not yet a critical mass of the American body politic that believes the threat from their political opponents to be so profound that it requires such drastic action. The fury and rage one finds in political Twitter and in political journals haven't quite yet permeated the larger culture.

Make no mistake, American political rhetoric is all too often just as apocalyptic as the rhetoric in more divided times. Proposed changes in health care laws will allegedly "kill thousands." The most hysterical voices even describe *tax cuts* as potentially deadly. The political atmosphere has grown so menacing that virtually any person who steps into the public square can expect to experience the worst kind of hate speech and even death threats.

But that sense of menace and danger hasn't traveled far beyond the political classes, at least not yet. That may well change, however, and it could change soon. The fall of 2018 witnessed a number of terrifying far-right hate crimes. An anti-Semite walked into a Pittsburgh synagogue and killed eleven worshippers. A white supremacist attempted to attack an African American church, and when he couldn't get in the door he turned his guns on black shoppers at a grocery store in Kentucky. He killed two before an armed citizen stopped his killing spree. In Florida, another far-right terrorist gunned down two women as part of a bizarre misogynist terror campaign.

The violence continued in 2019. In Poway, California, a white nationalist attempted to massacre worshippers in a synagogue. In El Paso, Texas, a white nationalist entered a Walmart, intentionally targeted those he believed to be Mexican, and killed twenty-two innocent men, women, and children. By the time this book is published, the list is likely to be even longer.

And the violence hasn't been confined to the right. Incidents of right-wing terrorism came on the heels of ricin scares directed at Republican senators, and for every example of right-wing thuggery online, conservatives could pull up images of far-left antifa (so-called anti-fascist) gangs hiding behind black masks as they viciously beat journalists and sometimes even conservative bystanders. And we cannot forget the attempted large-scale assassination of Republican members of Congress at a baseball field in Virginia.

Social media and ubiquitous smartphones amplify every incident. If an antifa thug beats up a conservative journalist, the video will receive millions of views overnight. At the same time, if a Trump supporter assaults a protester at a rally, a video of that incident will spread with extraordinary speed—but in an entirely different ideological corner of the internet.

The end result is that both sides receive direct evidence of violence inflicted on their allies but are often entirely unaware of violence inflicted on their opponents. So the narrative builds. "They" are violent. "They" are dangerous. And "we" are innocent.

Is there a level of violence that could start to break America? I believe so, and I believe America is capable of sliding into that level of violence. I also know we don't have to look all that far back into our history to see how political differences can spiral into systematic, pervasive, and terrifying domestic strife.

Our memories are short. We've already forgotten the sheer amount of violent conflict that stained American life during the Vietnam War.

A 2009 *New York Times* story reflecting back on the sixties called 1969 the "year of the bomb" and related stunning Senate findings on the extent of political violence: "From January 1969 to April 1970, the United States sustained 4,330 bombings—3,355 of them incendiary, 975 explosive—resulting in 43 deaths and $21.8 million in property damage."[1] And that's just one measure of violence across one fifteen-month span of time. Throughout much of the sixties and early seventies, there was large-scale campus unrest, including campus takeovers by armed students, arson, and significant property damage. There was an infamous National Guard shooting at Kent State University. The campuses, however, were peaceful compared to America's big cities. There were race riots from coast to coast, in virtually every region in the United States. Some—like the Detroit riot—required military intervention to suppress. The Detroit riot alone claimed forty-three lives. More than 1,400 buildings were burned and 1,700 stores looted.

President Johnson appointed a National Advisory Commission on Civil Disorders, known as the Kerner Commission, and it identified "more than 150 riots or major disorders between 1965 and 1968. In 1967 alone, 83 people were killed and 1,800 were injured—the majority of them African Americans—and property valued at more than $100 million was damaged, looted or destroyed."[2]

The commission also wrote these famous words: "Our nation is moving toward two societies, one black, one white—separate and unequal. Reaction to last summer's disorders has quickened the movement and deepened the division. Discrimination and segregation have long permeated much of American life; they now threaten the future of every American."[3]

We also cannot forget the string of assassinations and attempted assassinations that plagued American life. John F. Kennedy's assassination in 1963 of course traumatized the nation. But so did the April 1968 assassination of Martin Luther King Jr. and the June 1968 assassination of Robert Kennedy.

By many measures there was far more unrest and violence in the sixties and seventies than in the run-up to the Civil War. Even "Bleeding Kansas" didn't bleed from political violence as much as America's cities did in 1967. Yet our nation didn't fracture. It didn't come close to fracturing.

Why not?

Let's look back at the four factors that led to southern secession and apply them to the 1960s and early 1970s. First, the areas of unrest were not geographically contiguous. They were scattered across the nation. Second, that scattering prevented the formation of a geographically concentrated cultural critical mass.

As a consequence, while there was considerable fear that American culture was under threat (the third factor), and many Americans feared for their lives (the fourth factor), the lack of a geographic center prevented a terrorist crime wave from transforming into a true secessionist insurrection.

The only possible exception to this analysis was the "massive resistance" to integration that was located in the rump of the old Confederacy and featured official violence, mob violence, terror, and murder directed against African Americans. But a fragment of an already defeated state was never going to be strong enough, large enough, or determined enough to repeat the grave error of 1861.

To emphasize the lack of a geographically contiguous, culturally homogenous dissenting bloc, look no further than the results of twenty years' worth of presidential elections. After the divisiveness of 1968, four of the next five presidential elections were extraordinary landslides—elections unthinkable in our polarized present. In 1972, Nixon won 49 states and 520 electoral votes. In 1980, Ronald Reagan won 45 states and 489 electoral votes. He followed that up with his 1984 triumph, a 49-state win with a stunning 525 electoral votes. In 1988, even the less popular George H. W. Bush was able to win a margin no one has been able to achieve since—a 41-state win with 426 electoral votes. And while there was certainly divided government during that period (the Democrats held the House throughout all the years of GOP presidential dominance), there was unthinkable—by today's standards—national public consensus around the office of the president.

In other words, the fear and violence of the sixties did indeed trigger a reaction, but it was a national reaction, not a regional reaction, and that national reaction resulted in a far greater degree of national unity than we enjoy today. The length of time between the "year of the bomb" and Ronald Reagan's triumphant "Morning in America" reelection landslide was a short fifteen years.

Try to imagine this level of violence in the age of Twitter and the hot take. Not only do we spend days allocating blame over individual shootings or civil disturbances, but even small acts like an entirely peaceful confrontation on the steps of the Lincoln Memorial between Catholic kids from a Kentucky boys' school and a Native American elder can lead to angry rhetoric, death threats, and attempts to ruin the livelihoods of the boys' parents.

Now, imagine that same culture, except with a political bombing every few *hours*.

The Americans of today are not inherently better or inherently more peaceful than the Americans of fifty years ago. We are polarized, yes, but we have not also experienced that polarization in the midst of an event as divisive and deadly as the Vietnam War (where American draftees experienced casualties at rates that exceeded the casualty rates of the war on terror by several orders of magnitude) or a social upheaval as dramatic as the civil rights movement.

In other words, until the coronavirus recession, we had enjoyed the luxury of experiencing the worst waves of mutual enmity against a backdrop of relative peace and prosperity. But what if our mutual enmity gets worse? Won't that make America more prone to violence? Won't that magnify the impact of any given political crisis on our national union?

Of course it will, and if there is one thing you can count on for the foreseeable future, it's that our divisions are almost certain to grow.

How an Academic Paper
Explains America

When I speak around the country about our nation's dangerous polarization, I tell the audience if they can remember one thing from my talk, it should be an obscure academic paper written in 1999 by University of Chicago law professor Cass Sunstein. Better than anything else I've read, it explains why the geographic separations I tracked above have such a practical, malignant effect on American politics.

That paper is called "The Law of Group Polarization," and when you read it, you get one of those eureka moments that explains so much about our present world.[1] Puzzling events start to make sense. So, just as I tell my live audiences: If you read only one chapter in this book, this is the chapter to read. If you understand only one concept in this book, understand Sunstein's argument.

In his paper, Sunstein examined what he calls the "standard premise" that group deliberation leads to better outcomes. In other words, do we really make more reasonable decisions when we consult with groups of people? The obvious answer would seem to be yes. After all, it's in discussions with groups that we test the weaknesses of our ideas, encounter better suggestions, and refine our thoughts. This makes intuitive sense. It makes biblical sense. Proverbs 15:22 famously states, "Plans fail for lack of counsel, but with many advisers they succeed."

How many times have you gone to friends to discuss a career challenge—or a family problem—and come away from the conversation with a new perspective or perhaps tempered enthusiasm? I've never met a good parent who hasn't spent countless hours consulting with other family members, friends, counselors, or pastors about the challenge of raising children. I've never made a single job change or serious life change without seeking advice from the people closest to me. In many ways, it's life malpractice not to deliberate in groups.

Here's the important qualification, however. When I seek advice, I know that I'm seeking it from people who won't simply tell me what I want to hear. They'll have different perspectives on my decision. We may be bound together by love for one another, but the different members of the group have different life experiences, and I know they won't be afraid to tell me if they think I'm making a bad decision.

But what if the group begins with what Sunstein calls a "predeliberation tendency"? In other words, what if they begin with a bias? What if you're not working with people who have a diversity of views but, rather, you're deliberating with people of like mind? In that case, Sunstein says, "in a striking empirical regularity, deliberation tends to move groups, and the individuals who compose them, toward a more extreme point in the direction indicated by their own predeliberation judgments."

That's rather dry academic language (Sunstein was

writing a law and economics paper, after all), but here's what it means in plain English: when people of like mind gather, they tend to become more extreme. Sunstein offers a number of examples. If professors supportive of affirmative action gather to exchange ideas and plan next steps, aren't they likely to be even more strongly supportive of affirmative action and more likely to engage in activism after they meet?

Similarly, if a group that generally favors gun control meets to discuss a policy response to a recent horrific school shooting, won't their individual views tend to move more to the left on gun policy?

Think of your own life. If you support the Second Amendment and you gather with friends who also oppose restrictions on gun rights, do your group conversations tend to moderate each person's views? Or, as I've put it when speaking to church groups about group polarization, does a good worship service or good Bible study generally make you love Jesus *less*?

Indeed, the predeliberation bias can strongly impact even those who don't share the bias, if they're in a small enough minority. This can happen even when the group bias is clearly and obviously wrong. For example, as Sunstein relates, an experiment conducted by a social psychologist named Solomon Asch indicated that in certain circumstances—when the peer pressure is severe enough—"individuals were willing to abandon the direct evidence of their own senses."

In the Asch experiments, groups were given different cards with lines on them and asked to match lines of the same length. Some lines were obviously a perfect match. Others were obviously not. In normal circumstances, the subjects of the experiment made a mistake "less than 1 percent of the time." But then Asch introduced a twist. Virtually the entire group—who were collaborating with the researcher—made an intentional, deliberate mistake, choosing a line that was obviously not the correct length. The single subject was then left to decide on their own whether to make the correct choice. What happened? Here's Sunstein:

> In rounds in which group pressure supported the incorrect answer, subjects erred 36.8% of the time. Indeed, in a series of twelve questions, no less than 70% of subjects went along with the group, and defied the evidence of their own senses, at least once.

In other words, group pressure—the predeliberation tendency—was so strong that individuals would rather be clearly wrong than clearly alone.

When I read Sunstein's paper, I immediately recalled an incident in my own high school. Our school's psychology teacher performed a version of the test to demonstrate the awesome power of peer pressure to bend students to its will. He gathered together a small group of the most popular students in school—the point guard on the basketball team, several cheerleaders, the homecoming king and queen—and put them on a panel.

Ten students were asked to come to the classroom. I was one of them. Those of us in this group waited outside as, one by one, we were ushered inside. I had absolutely no idea what was going on. Then it was my turn. I sat next to the cheerleaders while the teacher held up cards with two lines on them. He asked, "Which one is longer?" One by one the panelists went down the line and called out the answer. I was last.

The first four or five cards were obvious, and everyone got the correct answer. Then one of the cards was close and the group's opinions were mixed. I peered at the card and answered as best I could. For the next card the lines were very close, and every other person answered the same way, but their answer was incorrect. I'll never forget leaning forward to look at the lines while a substantial portion of the cheerleading squad looked at me with some variation of contempt or disgust.

I gave the correct answer, but I felt bad about it. I said it apologetically, in the way an insecure nerd tries to be correct without being annoying. After it was all over, the teacher told us that it was a "stacked" peer pressure test: he'd asked the panelists to look as annoyed and condescending as possible, and student after student had gone along with the crowd.

When I tell this story, everyone nods. That's high school peer pressure. That's corporate groupthink. At some point in our lives virtually every one of us has gone along with the crowd when the opinions of the crowd matter to us and when we perceive risk in defying its judgment. At worst, we enthusiastically participate. Sometimes our silence constitutes effective consent. It's hard to be our best selves and risk shame in the peer groups that matter most.

All of this is true, but then Sunstein goes further. He introduces the concept of the "cascade"—when "individuals and social groups sometimes move quite rapidly in some direction or another." Pardon the lengthy quote from Sunstein, but I can't improve on his explanation. Here's how a cascade occurs:

> If A is unaware whether abandoned toxic waste dumps are in fact hazardous, he may be moved in the direction of fear if B seems to think that fear is justified. If A and B believe that fear is justified, C may end up thinking so too, at least if she lacks independent information to the contrary. If A, B, and C believe that abandoned hazardous waste dumps are hazardous, D will have to have a good deal of confidence to reject their shared conclusion. The result of this process can be to produce cascade effects, as large groups of people end up believing something—even if that something is false—simply because other people seem to believe it too. There is a great deal of experimental evidence of informational cascades, which are easy to induce in the laboratory; real world phenomena also seem to have a great deal to do with cascade effects. Notice here that when a cascade is occurring, large numbers of persons end up with a shared view, not simply because of social influence, but via a particular process, in which a rivulet ends up as a flood.

Compare these concepts to American political discourse. Talk to many Americans, and they assume that political views are held in something like a bell curve. There's a large middle—that's the "center right" and the "center left"—with a small number of people at either end. So when they see particularly offensive arguments from their political opponents, they often console themselves that those arguments are from a "fringe." Most people, they believe, are relatively moderate.

This is getting less true every day. At the risk of throwing too much data at you, let's refer to the Pew Research Center's indispensable study of American polarization.[2] The bell curve is getting smashed into a blob; the rivulet of people moving to the edges of discourse is becoming a flood. Between 1994 and 2017, the bell curve started to flatten, and both sides were responsible for the change— both sides were growing more extreme at roughly the same rate.

Is it a coincidence that this ideological polarization is occurring at exactly the same time as the "big sort"? Is it a coincidence that this ideological polarization is happening just as we hit a record number of landslide counties in the 2016 election?

Keep in mind, this polarization isn't just about party identity, it's about *ideas*. Yes, America is negatively polarized—we hate the other team more than we love our own—but it's ideologically polarized as well. Even if we could somehow grow to like a person on the other side, we would have to overcome or overlook a broader ideological divide than in years past.

Indeed, negative polarization feeds ideological polarization, as we stampede to take views opposite to the ones our hated foes hold. The idea gap directly impacts the likability gap, and the likability gap impacts the idea gap, creating the worst kind of negative feedback loop of fear and alienation. A person can have a high degree of character, kindness, and personal integrity, but if they hold to ideas at odds with the opposition, they'll be demonized and vilified as morally defective—often with more vitriol than if their failings were "merely" personal.

To be clear, when I say that views are becoming more extreme, that is not to say that they're inherently illegitimate or inherently wrong. Some of the best American ideas were once extreme. Abolition was once an extremist position. Integration was once an extremist position. Women's suffrage was once an extremist position. There are countless examples where the mainstream started out as a virtuous extreme.

But regardless of the virtue of the underlying positions, it is a simple fact that when *both* sides move to their own edges—regardless of the virtue of that edge—it exacerbates division, and the fact of that division in the United States today is growing increasingly impossible to deny.

Churches and Cities, the Core of Group Polarization

So far the discussion of group polarization has been more theoretical than practical. But what does polarization look like in practice? Which key American communities suffer from such decisive "predeliberation tendencies" that the group dynamic can overwhelm individual dissent and create exactly the "cascade" that Sunstein described? There are many. Here are two—the white Evangelical church and urban progressive enclaves.

First, let me talk about my tribe—white Evangelicals. I'm a reformed Presbyterian. I attend a conservative Presbyterian church, I graduated from a Christian college, and there is not a day in my life when I don't remember believing that Jesus is Lord. I'm pro-life, pro-religious liberty, and at one point I had sued more American universities than any other living lawyer to protect free speech and religious freedom on campus.

And yet there were moments in the 2016 election when I scarcely recognized my own neighbors and longtime friends. If you want to talk about cascades, the Evangelical cascade not just to Republicans in general but to Donald Trump in particular was a sight to behold.

Make no mistake, since at least 2004 white Evangelicals have decisively turned their backs on the Democrats. John Kerry got only 21 percent of the Evangelical vote. Barack Obama got 24 percent and 21 percent in 2008 and 2012, respectively. In 2016, however, Hillary Clinton received the support of only 16 percent of Evangelicals. Trump—the thrice-married, philandering man who paid hush money to a porn star and rarely darkened the door of a church—received a whopping 81 percent of the Evangelical vote.[1] That's a gap eight points greater than devout Christian George W. Bush enjoyed in his campaign against John Kerry.

So how did Evangelicals come to support Trump in spite of his many and manifest character flaws? One answer is of course pure partisanship. The vast majority of white Evangelicals are Republicans, and Republicans back Republicans. But I'd submit that something deeper was at work in 2016. I'd submit that for white Evangelicals to overwhelmingly support a Republican so different from every other GOP nominee in the modern era, some *ideas* had to change, and the fact that they did change—and so quickly—is evidence of exactly the preference cascade that Sunstein describes.

But let's back up. In 1998, at the height of the impeachment battle against Bill Clinton, the Southern Baptist Convention issued a Resolution on Moral Character of Public Officials.[2] It's a short document, and its meaning is clear. It lamented the fact that "many Americans are willing to excuse or overlook immoral or illegal conduct by unrepentant public officials so long as economic prosperity prevails," and it followed up with a clear and unequivocal theological statement, one familiar to any person with even a passing familiarity with the Old Testament: "Tolerance of serious wrong by leaders sears the conscience of the culture, spawns unrestrained immorality and lawlessness in the society, and surely results in God's judgment."

Let's put this plainly. The Southern Baptists were asserting that no matter the secular outcome of a president's terms (for example, peace and prosperity), if the culture tolerates "serious wrong," then divine judgment "surely" comes. Who wants to risk divine judgment?

So this means Evangelicals were most concerned about the character of leaders, correct? This means that at least a decent level of honesty and integrity was a prerequisite for Evangelical support, right? It seemed so, and for a time Evangelical political values seemed to reflect this theological orthodoxy.

For example, in a 2011 poll, Evangelicals were the American religious subgroup least likely to say that "an elected official who commits an immoral act in their personal life can still behave ethically and fulfill their duties in their public and professional life." Only 30 percent agreed, compared to 38 percent of mainline Protestants, 42 percent of Catholics, and 63 percent of unaffiliated Americans.

By 2016, Evangelicals had flipped. They outraced secular Americans to be the religious group *most* likely to accept an elected official who commits an immoral act in their personal life.[3]

Let's call this the King David cascade. If you followed it in real time, the dynamic happened exactly as Sunstein outlined when he described the process of producing "cascade effects." The King David cascade went something like this:

Person A: God has used terribly flawed kings to accomplish his purposes. David had a man killed. Nothing Trump has done approaches that level of depravity.

Person B: I see your point. It's not as if God declared that because of David's sins he'd back the Philistines.

Person C: Just like we can read the Psalms without believing David's affair with Bathsheba was moral, I can support Trump's policies without excusing his decadence.

And it wasn't just the King David comparisons. Those who rejected the David analogy (and there were many who did; after all, King David repented of his sins, and Trump is notorious for believing he does little wrong) had other biblical examples to appeal to. There was Cyrus the Great, the Persian king who ended the Israelites' captivity and directed the rebuilding of the Temple in Jerusalem. If the Lord could use a pagan king to serve a great purpose, could he not use a nominal Presbyterian to accomplish his will?

There were also the references to the (possibly apocryphal) Martin Luther quote "I'd rather be ruled by a wise Turk than by a foolish Christian"—especially when the "foolish Christian" (Clinton) sought public funding for abortions and was hostile to religious liberty.

As Sunstein said, a rivulet becomes a flood.

The overwhelming predeliberation tendency was toward the GOP, the challenge to the tendency was Donald Trump, and the law of group polarization locked in to reinforce the tendency and move the population quickly and massively into a fundamentally changed position— one, incidentally, that the opposing side found particularly infuriating.

But lest we unfairly pick on the right, no one should pretend the left isn't plagued by its own cascades— particularly its secular social justice cascades. There has been an undeniable, rapid evolution of left-wing thinking along a number of cultural and political fronts.

If you don't think there's a predeliberation tendency on the left, you're not paying attention. In my years living in places like New York City, Cambridge, Massachusetts, and Center City Philadelphia, I've heard countless progressives mock Evangelicals for their "groupthink" and their "herd mentality." Yet it's a simple fact that many urban centers are less politically diverse than your average Evangelical megachurch.

In fact, a white Republican attending church is often more likely to meet a Democrat than a progressive living in Manhattan is likely to meet a Republican. All the progressives I know (and, for that matter, all the conservatives I know) think of themselves as free, independent thinkers. The progressives I know, however, are much *more* likely to think of themselves as transgressive or noncomformist. They're anything but. Let's look at some numbers, and as you do, remember that in 2016 Evangelicals voted for Trump by a margin of 81 percent to 16 percent.

> San Francisco voted for Clinton over Trump by a margin of 84 percent to 9 percent.[4]
> The Bronx voted for Clinton over Trump by 88 percent to 10 percent.[5]
> Manhattan voted for Clinton over Trump by 86 percent to 10 percent.[6]
> Washington, D.C., gave a stunning 91 percent of its votes to Clinton.[7]
> Philadelphia County voted for Clinton over Trump by 82 percent to 15 percent.[8]

This is a remarkable level of ideological uniformity. Yes, there are variations within the progressive mainstream—like there are denominations within Evangelicalism—but this overwhelming consensus creates any number of pre-deliberation tendencies. This is your liberal bubble. This is your progressive cocoon.

If you live much of your life online, it's easy to see how quickly cultural ideas evolve on the left side of the spectrum. Once-beloved television shows—including shows written by progressives, directed by progressives, and starring progressives—are now problematic to progressives. Just read some of the commentary surrounding shows like *Friends* or even *Sex and the City*. Concepts like "trigger warnings," "microaggressions," and "cultural appropriation" have exploded from the extreme quarters of the academy to the mainstream of progressive thought with stunning speed.

Sure, some of these developments represent fringe fads more than they do any sort of sea change. People still watch and enjoy *Friends*, and often the essays and hashtags that launch each new facet of identity politics are met with sighs and eye rolls by more sober-minded leaders on the left. But it is still true that new trends in racial and sexual politics are emerging with stunning speed.

I don't want to focus on these easy targets, however. Online trends move so quickly that blazing controversies of 2018 or 2019 will sound dated by 2020. Instead, I want to focus on an aspect of group polarization that is far, far more consequential—an aspect that stands to separate Americans more than sometimes silly debates about classroom syllabi and whether Scarlett Johansson can play a transgender man or an Asian woman in her movies. I'm talking about the rapid secularization of white progressives.

For a largely Christian country committed since its founding to religious liberty, it's disheartening to see the hostility against Christianity in many progressive enclaves—especially when orthodox Christianity butts heads with the political movement for LGBT rights that is so vital to many progressive Americans.

By this point, the stories are so frequent and so commonly debated that they're hardly worth repeating. If a conservative state enacts religious liberties legislation, progressive companies routinely threaten to boycott. If a Christian student group enacts rules of sexual conduct for its leaders, it routinely risks expulsion from campus. Obama administration gender-identity directives—requiring educators to use chosen pronouns, allow trans boys and girls to compete in sports according to their identity (and not their sex), and grant access to bathrooms and other private spaces on the basis of identity—spawned multiple federal lawsuits.

Time and again, these disputes aren't the result of debates between different strands of Christianity, but rather the result of conflict between religious and secular Americans, with secular Americans clustered in very specific geographic and ideological enclaves and subject to very powerful group dynamics.

Elite secularization is so out of hand that it's ripe for parody—at least by independent-minded thinkers who don't mind a little pop culture blowback.

I'm thinking of an episode of the late and lamented Mike Judge comedy *Silicon Valley*. The gang at Pied Piper (the fictional tech startup at the heart of the series) was assembling a coalition of companies to use its new product, but it ran into a problem. One of the CEOs was—gasp—a Christian. He was gay and ran a gays-only dating app, but he went to church regularly.[9] The show's protagonist, Richard Hendricks, accidentally "outed" him as a person of faith, then spent the rest of the show trying to contain the damage. In Silicon Valley, "you can be openly polyamorous, and people will call you brave," one character explained. "You can put microdoses of LSD in your cereal, and people will call you a pioneer. But the one thing you cannot be is a Christian." Or, as the gay Christian laments, "My dad says my lifestyle makes him sick. He just wants his gay son back."

The show's humor was based in more than a kernel of truth. In 2018, the Pew Research Center (yes, I know, more Pew) released survey results showing an immense

"God gap" between white Republicans and white Democrats. While 72 percent of white Republicans believed in the "God of the Bible," only 32 percent of white Democrats shared their faith.[10]

The first and most obvious explanation for this gap isn't a Sunstein cascade but rather simple sorting. Based on party platforms and ideologies, aren't secular people likely to leave the Republican Party and move over to the Democrats? Aren't religious Democrats more likely to become Republican?

If that's true, you'd expect the percentage of religious Republicans to rise at the same time that the share of religious Democrats dropped. That does not appear to be the case, however.

Between 2004 and 2016—a mere twelve years—the percentage of white Democrats who said religion is important in their lives fell from roughly 70 percent to well under 50 percent. Nor was this a case of religious Democrats becoming Republicans. The Republican numbers held steady. And the decrease was not a simple generational phenomenon. Again, younger Republican numbers held steady. Among younger Democrats, the share collapsed to close to 30 percent.

Why would we see such a collapse? After all, the same Pew data indicate that a God gap exists not just between white Republicans and white Democrats, but between white Democrats and black Democrats. Republicans and black Democrats have extremely similar religious beliefs and religious habits.

It appears, however, that this largely white, secular cohort represents the most energized element of the Democratic coalition. Writing in *The Atlantic* in October

2018, Emma Green explained the power of this very active group:

> In [a Public Religion Research Institute] survey of 1,811 respondents, conducted this year in August and September, religiously unaffiliated Democrats were more than twice as likely to have attended a rally within the past 12 months compared with their religious peers. During that time, they were significantly more likely to have contacted an elected official or to have donated to a candidate or cause. And nearly half of religiously unaffiliated Democrats said they had bought or boycotted a product for political reasons or posted political opinions online, compared with roughly one-quarter of their religious peers.[11]

Think of these factors in light of the Sunstein concepts. A motivated segment of the group is exerting pressure in the group deliberations, and the group as a whole is responding—even in the context of the most vital questions of life, death, heaven, and hell. The law of group polarization is so strong that it can change religious beliefs. It can alter faith practices on a large scale.

7

Politics Trumps Everything

A nd that brings me to the next question. Exactly how powerful is the dark magic of group polarization? Would you believe me if I told you that there is now evidence that political affiliation is becoming so important that for some people it is trumping *every other aspect* of their identity? Imagine if the GOP was so tied to a white Christian identity that even non-white, non-Christian members of the party were more apt to identify as white and Christian. Or, conversely, what if the Democrats were so entrenched as a secular, racially and sexually diverse party that members of the party changed how they described themselves to better match their political in-group?

Surely group polarization isn't that strong, is it? It may well be, at least for some people. In September 2018, New York University political scientist Patrick Egan released a paper demonstrating that "some liberal Democrats and conservative Republicans shift their identities to better align with the demographic prototypes of their political groups."[1] In other words, "small but significant shares of Americans engage in identity switching with regard to ethnicity, religion, sexual orientation, and class that is predicted by partisanship and ideology in their pasts, bringing their identities into better alignment with their politics."[2]

There are some Latino Republicans who functionally shed their Latino identity. There are gay Republicans who shed their LGBT identity. There are religious Democrats who shed their faith and white Democrats who strain to find a non-white ethnic identity. Demographic differences are so well known in American politics that the two sides often "substantially exaggerate them in their minds."

For example, Republicans think almost half of Democrats are black. The real number is 24 percent. They think a whopping 38 percent are lesbian, gay, or bisexual. The real number is 6 percent. They also think 44 percent of Democrats are union members. The real number is 11 percent.[3]

Democrats aren't quite as misguided about Republicans, but they still get several characteristics substantially wrong. They think 44 percent of Republicans are sixty-five or older. The real number is 21 percent. They think 44 percent are Evangelical and 44 percent are southern. The real numbers are 34 and 36 percent, respectively. The most colossal swing and miss, however, came when Democrats estimated Republican incomes. They guessed that 44 percent of Republicans made $250,000 or more per year. The real number? A mere 2 percent.[4]

Reporting on these numbers for the website FiveThirty-Eight (as part of its excellent coverage of America's partisan divides), writer Perry Bacon Jr. spotlighted the role of politics in creating a "mega-identity" that subsumes all other identities. He highlights this passage from political scientist Lilliana Mason's book *Uncivil Agreement: How Politics Became Our Identity*:

> A single vote can now indicate a person's partisan preference *as well* as his or her religion, race, ethnicity, gender, neighborhood and favorite grocery store. This is no longer a single social identity. Partisanship can now be thought of as a mega-identity, with all of the psychological and behavioral magnifications that implies.

This means, as Bacon explains, that telling a person about any one aspect of your identity tells them far less about you than simply telling them whether you're a Republican or a Democrat. For example, if you told them that you are a Republican, "they could reasonably assume that you are not black, lesbian, gay, transgender or bisexual, nonreligious or Jewish."[5]

Moving back to Egan's paper, is it any wonder then that with mega-identities so strong, "the process of self-categorization leads some people to adopt identities that conform with these prototypes and shed identities that do not"?

It's easy for some of us to look at this reality and scoff. You mean some people are so serious about politics that they'll strain to be more or less white, more or less religious to fit in with their political tribe? How pitiful. Have some self-respect.

But we cannot and must not forget human nature. We cannot and must not forget the deep and profound need for human companionship. In his book *Them*, Nebraska senator Ben Sasse discusses the incredible power of loneliness in American society. We are "social, relational" beings, he says. We need tribes, but—he argues—too many of the tribes that have sustained us are in a state of collapse. Families fracture, Americans disconnect from civic institutions and church attendance, and stable jobs are harder to find. It's hard to find a sustainable, thriving community of friends and colleagues. So we seek connection. We seek a sense of belonging and purpose.

Many millions of us find that sense of belonging and purpose in politics. Our political identity truly defines our tribe. Thus it is no wonder that some of us would shed or minimize identities that make us feel on the edges of our most cherished in-group. It's no wonder that we'd be susceptible to the social pressures of that group and stampede toward the perceived consensus.

And it's the very collapse of other cultural and tribal institutions that is going to make our group polarization so very difficult to stop. We can't rebuild the family overnight, and multi-generation family fragmentation means that tens of millions of Americans don't know what a functioning nuclear family even looks like. They have no experience with family stability. None.

And what of our economic stability? I wrote this book in a time of economic prosperity. I finished it just as the coronavirus recession began, dramatically exacerbating economic anxiety. As Sasse notes, Americans are broadly divided into three main groups: the mobile, the rooted, and the stuck.

The mobile can and do take advantage of new opportunities. They can and do move to new jobs. The rooted are the kind of people who can move but choose to stay. They *want* to remain where they are and build lasting communities. The stuck have no choice. Even if they wanted to leave to build a new life, they can't.

"In the U.S.," Sasse says, "the mobile and the stuck categories are growing, while the rooted are rapidly dwindling."[6] If you're stuck, you're frustrated. If you're moving, your "place" is all too often determined by your phone, your computer, and your online life. We were not created to live like that. Our previous communities existed for deep and profound reasons.

What do we have left? Well, we have our politics, and—as we have seen—we run away from our opponent. We define ourselves by opposition. We're united by our loathing.

From Extreme to Mainstream, Time and Again

In his essay, Sunstein posits a form of group polarization that he says (writing, remember, in 1999) that he's not yet seen in studies. According to the logic of his theory, however, "group polarization suggests that if participants engage in repeated discussions—if, for example, they meet each month, express views, and take votes—there should be repeated shifts toward, and past, the defined pole." This means that "deliberation over time should produce a situation in which individuals hold positions more extreme than those of any individual member before the series of deliberations began."

In other words, Sunstein posited that group polarization could grow so profound that, given enough time, *entire groups* could grow more extreme than the most extreme member at the commencement of the movement.

I'd suggest to Sunstein that we do now have a study that confirms his theory, and that study is American politics. Let's consider sexual politics. I was a student at the very liberal Harvard Law School from 1991 to 1994. The time that's passed since is a small slice of our nation's history. So small, in fact, that not only do we debate today many of the same issues we debated then, but we even argue about some of the same politicians—Bill and Hillary Clinton, most notably.

But in those short years there has been a staggering change in attitudes about fundamental cultural values. In three years of heated debates about marriage and sexuality during my time in law school, I don't recall a single person arguing that, for example, a politician should be disqualified from running as a Democrat if he or she opposed gay marriage. I don't recall a single person arguing that Title IX protected the right of boys who identify as girls to participate in girls' sports. And I certainly don't recall a single person who would argue that it was a violation of federal civil rights law if you didn't call a transgender person by their preferred pronouns.

Yet each of these positions is now fundamentally mainstream on the left. It is odd to meet a progressive on a college campus—including a progressive my age—who doesn't agree wholeheartedly with each of these propositions. In other words, the entire group has migrated to a position more extreme than the most extreme position of individuals when the deliberations began.

Ask a conservative if they're winning the culture war, and they're likely to immediately say no. Religious liberty is under siege, isn't it? Traditional sexual morality is mocked and scorned, right? Traditional Christians are often despised and discriminated against in the academy, Hollywood, and progressive corporate America, aren't they? But there's a very notable exception to conservative losses: gun culture.

Here, the law of group polarization has worked in Republican circles to create an immense, unyielding coalition that works every bit as tirelessly to secure and expand gun rights as the cultural left works tirelessly to secure and expand sexual liberty. And, like the movement for LGBT equality, the gun rights movement has won in a rout.

While it's hard to pinpoint the launch of the modern gun rights revolution, let's go back to 1986, the year before the symbolic mass same-sex wedding ceremony on the National Mall in Washington. At that time, gun rights were restricted at a scale younger Americans simply wouldn't recognize. A majority of states (thirty-one) had either "no issue" or "may issue" rules for carry permits, meaning that a majority of states did not grant their citizens a right to carry a gun in self-defense outside the home.[1]

Ten years later, that number had flipped. Thirty states were "shall issue" states. In other words, citizens had a right to a carry permit so long as they could meet certain basic requirements, like passing a background check and attending a state-mandated class. One state, Vermont, was "constitutional carry." There were no restrictions on carrying a gun, provided you could own one legally.

Going back to my law school days, I was a broad supporter of gun rights, but I'd never even heard of constitutional carry. I was one of the most conservative students at the school, but I wouldn't have even known to argue that the Second Amendment was my carry permit.

Fast-forward to 2017, and there were a total of twenty-nine "shall issue" states, thirteen states that effectively had "constitutional carry," and only eight states with "may issue" rules. There were zero "no issue" states. Thirty years before, there had been sixteen, including— believe it or not—the state of Texas.

In theory, the gun rights movement and the movement for LGBT equality aren't at all incompatible with national unity. Many LGBT Americans proudly pack a pistol. But since the fight for LGBT rights has largely come from the left, and the gun rights movement has largely existed on the right, the reality of the two cultural movements has been to create two different communities who glare at each other from across a vast cultural and ideological divide, with little understanding of opposing views.

Constitutional carry, really? Have you lost your mind?

Multiple genders? Are you serious?

The Sunstein theory is so thoroughly vindicated that it's self-evidently true. When like-minded people gather, they tend to grow more extreme. The group will sometimes grow more extreme than the most extreme member. The result, over time, has been a flattening of the American bell curve. The left moves left, and the right moves right. We are moving away from each other at increasing speed.

By itself, group polarization presents an obvious challenge for national unity. Combine it with the "big sort," and you have people living in geographically contiguous, increasingly culturally homogenous regions of the country, sharing ever more extreme views. This is a recipe for polarization, but is it a recipe for actual division—especially in a nation that is otherwise bound together by strong bonds of shared history and (though strained) shared culture?

No, not necessarily. Here is where classical liberalism comes back into our story. Here is where the vision of the Founders can and should apply. Remember, the Founders were knitting together a country that comprised a variety of churches representing the theological and battlefield combatants in Europe's wars of religion—at a time when denominational differences weren't treated so much as good-faith deviations from otherwise solid orthodoxy than as tickets to eternal damnation. Religious division had eternal consequences.

Rather than seek the domination of one faith over the other, the one formal legal structure they put in place guaranteed the protection of competing faiths. Rather than use the constitutional convention and the ratification process to launch a culture war, they created national governing documents, including the Bill of Rights, that protected the individual and associational rights of competing factions. And they did this even as they believed that some competing factions were so malignant that they could destroy the human soul.

The Founders understood that they could not create a union without protecting that liberty, that the quest for domination of one faction over the other would tear the young nation apart. We need to relearn this lesson. Instead, as we sprint away from each other, we are also scorning the very idea of pluralism itself and the legal doctrines and cultural norms that preserve and sustain our nation's distinct communities.

Pluralism, in other words, becomes to the pure partisan mind an instrument of injustice and civil liberties a barrier to progress. Because when one is righteous, the very existence of dissenting communities is proof that justice is thwarted and evil exists. And why should any person protect the existence of evil?

Not long ago I was at a unique meeting of Americans from left, right, and center who are deeply concerned about negative polarization. No, this wasn't the standard group of center-right and center-left politicians and pundits that you see at all the respectable gatherings. This group consisted of people on virtually every point in the political spectrum. The invite list was confidential—in part because it could be problematic for some individuals to be in the same room as other participants (unless they were engaged in heated debate). The conversations were completely off the record. It was fair to say that virtually the only thing that united the people in that room was a deep concern that our present political culture was breaking America.

To preserve the peace, we left the substantive issues by the wayside—there were no debates about abortion, LGBT rights, or gun control. Instead, we asked if there was a way to fight about those issues without the nature of the debate itself further fracturing the country. We asked if civility was still possible, if there were potential common constitutional concerns, and whether the best we could do was simply maintain the integrity of our democratic institutions until our nation was able to muddle through this period of profound division and emerge on the other side—more unified, with politics more like the relatively functional (by comparison) eighties and nineties, when politicians fought but the population was less consumed with bitterness and loathing.

The conversation was interesting and challenging, but because we sidelined specific issues, it might have left us more optimistic than perhaps the facts warranted. During an informal moment, one of the participants said that he thought the conference showed that the American conversation could, in fact, be more civil and respectful.

Left and right could, in fact, talk about weighty issues without immediately devolving into fury and recriminations.

I wanted to believe he was correct. I still believe he could be correct. But I knew that even the peace of that meeting—a meeting among people of like enough mind that we were willing to spend days together to address common concerns—was fragile, perhaps more fragile than the participants realized.

So I spoke up. I said that as much as I was encouraged by the meeting and encouraged by the genuine new friendships, I was still pessimistic. I still believed that our challenges were more profound than we realized. I said that there was one question that, if we even tried to debate it, could well destroy the group, end the new friendships, and put us right back in our familiar corners. This was a question that many (perhaps most) of the participants would think it absurd even to ask—because the answer was so obvious and the contrary position so mystifying or infuriating.

The question was simple: Is Caitlyn Jenner a woman?

The words hung there for a moment. We looked at each other, and I could see the wheels turning. Did they want to take up the challenge? Did they want to prove that we could have a discussion about gender identity that was every bit as civil as the genuine search for constitutional common ground that had dominated previous sessions? But no one took it up. No. We can't possibly talk about that. That question is truly beyond debate.

The Shifting Window
of Acceptable Discourse

Years ago I learned about an obscure term that circulated in conservative think-tank circles. It's more famous now, but still, if you use it outside the world of political junkies, no one will know what you're talking about. The term is "Overton window."[1]

Developed by the late Joseph Overton, a former vice president of the Mackinac Center for Public Policy, the "window" concept refers to the range of acceptable political discourse on any given topic.[2] As the Mackinac Center explains, "The 'window' of politically acceptable options is primarily defined not by what politicians prefer, but rather by what they believe they can support and still win re-election."[3] The key to shifting policy lies not so much in changing politicians but in changing the terms of the debate. In other words, "the window shifts to include different policy options not when ideas change among politicians, but when ideas change in the society that elects them."

The left—dominating the media, the academy, and pop culture—has been extraordinarily effective at moving the Overton window. As I noted in Chapter 8, the fight for gay marriage represents an extraordinary example of moving the window so dramatically that yesterday's conventional wisdom is today's bigotry. Just one generation ago gay marriage was a subject so far outside the mainstream that Republicans and Democrats united to overwhelmingly pass the Defense of Marriage Act (DOMA) to define marriage under federal law as the union of one man and one woman. Now? That view is such an anathema that it's difficult to get—or retain—a job in entire sectors of the economy if you openly hold to the traditionalist position on marriage.

By moving the Overton window, an ideological movement can "win" no matter the partisan outcome of the election. After all, if both sides consent to the cultural change, the issue is settled regardless of who wins the race. Going back to gay marriage, there is not a single serious national Republican politician who will try to reverse *Obergefell*. No one will run on that platform. No one will govern on that platform. No one will even pay lip service to that platform. Why? Because the entire framework for debate has shifted. A position once mainstream in both parties—and then mainstream in one party—now is no longer mainstream in either party.

In fact, the left's success at moving the window is one reason conservatives feel like they lose even when they win. If the left wins the culture and the right wins the statehouses, ultimately the left wins. Why? Because politics—to paraphrase the late conservative journalist Andrew Breitbart—is ultimately downstream from culture. It's American culture that defines the terms of American political debate.

To grasp more fully the conservative complaint, think

of the immense changes in American politics since Bill
Clinton's two terms. I'm old enough to remember how
conservative Americans were appalled by his election.
Here was a draft-dodging, pot-smoking libertine in the
Oval Office, married to a woman who only occasionally
took his name and openly scorned cookie-baking "stand
by your man" domesticity. In other words, the sixties
counterculture had triumphed, and now it was in the
White House.

Clinton certainly had some progressive impulses. He
was a reliable supporter of abortion rights, he nominated
progressive judges, and he diverted enormous amounts of
energy in his first term into a failed effort at health care
reform. But in other ways his administration was more
conservative than the modern GOP. As noted above, he
passed DOMA—a law that wouldn't even make it to
the House floor today. He passed the sweeping federal
Religious Freedom Restoration Act (RFRA)—another
law now so contentious that it couldn't possibly survive
a filibuster, even if the GOP was steadfast enough to
bring it to a vote.

That's not all. He passed a draconian crime bill that
was so tough that, again, not even the GOP would raise
it now. He was an aggressive hawk, striking Iraq, Sudan,
and Afghanistan. He intervened twice in the Balkans,
throwing American airpower into a vicious ethnic struggle and ultimately deploying troops to keep the peace.

Oh, and by the way, he was (with the help of the GOP-
controlled Congress) so fiscally restrained that by the end
of his second term, the United States was running an
extraordinary budget surplus.

For those keeping score, it's almost certain the

Overton window has moved so much that DOMA, RFRA, the Clinton crime bill, and—because of the fiscal restraint it would require—a budget surplus are outside the cultural confines of modern politics. That's the power of culture. That's the power of the Overton window.

It's at this point that conservatives nod in near-unison. For generations, conservatives believed—with very good reason—that we don't control our common culture, and that the left's hammerlock on the most important cultural institutions meant that we were fighting a perpetual rear-guard action. Those moving the left edge of the window were simply stronger than those on the right edge. America was moving left; the only question was the speed of the change.

That's what progressives called the "arc of history."

It's what conservatives called "defeat."

But things have changed. Yes, progressives still control most of the media, large sections of corporate America, and the academy. They run social media. Remember, however, the reality of our cultural separation. The media environment is far more fragmented, and conservatives can easily find niche programming that suits their tastes. And even though progressives run Facebook and Twitter, conservatives—especially on Facebook—are extraordinarily adept at using the platform to spread conservative messages.

It's a brave new world, and conservatives have adapted to it very well.

The result is that the forces pushing the right edge of the Overton window have grown so strong that on many issues they've pulled the window apart. There is no longer a single window; there are two. And negative polarization means that the two windows are moving away from each other so fast that it's now difficult to engage in even the most basic of good-faith conversations on some of the most critical issues that define American politics.

For example, let's go back to guns, and this time we'll discuss not so much gun policy as the near-impossibility of good-faith conversation about one of the most important cultural and political issues in the United States. On February 21, 2018—just one week after a horrifying school shooting claimed seventeen lives in Parkland, Florida— CNN conducted a town-hall-style debate about gun rights. Hosted by Jake Tapper, it was intended to be a respectful dialogue, where left and right could debate gun rights in good faith in front of grieving members of the community. But that's not what happened.[4]

Instead, the nation witnessed what looked a lot like an extended version of the famous Two Minutes Hate from George Orwell's novel *1984*. The shooting happened in a blue county, and the furious crowd jeered the two conservatives, Senator Marco Rubio and NRA spokesperson Dana Loesch, who stood in defense of the Second Amendment.

The crowd mocked the notion that rape victims might want to arm themselves for protection. There were calls of "murderer." Rubio was compared to a mass killer. There were wild cheers for the idea of banning every single semiautomatic rifle in America. The discourse was vicious. It was also slanderous. There were millions of gun-owning Americans who watched all or part of the town hall and came away with a clear message: These people aren't just angry at what happened in their town, to their friends and family members. They hate me. They really believe I'm the kind of person who doesn't care if kids die, and they want to deprive me of the ability to defend myself. And if they hate me, then they certainly don't want to hear what I have to say. Conversation is useless. Only power matters now.

The CNN town hall might in other circumstances have been easy to write off as an outlier, a result of the still-raw grief and pain left in the wake of the Parkland shooting. But it was no less vitriolic than the "discourse" online, where progressives who hadn't lost anyone in the attack were using many of the same words as the angry crowd that confronted Rubio and Loesch. The NRA has blood on its hands, they said. It's a terrorist organization. Gun rights supporters—especially those who oppose an assault weapons ban—are lunatics at best, evil at worst.

Unfortunately, there was a similar angry response from the nation's most powerful gun rights organization. The NRA's video channel, NRATV, put out a video that actually declared, "No one on this planet benefits more from mass shootings—and motivates more people to become mass shooters—than the mainstream media."[5] It continued, "The mainstream media love mass shootings." The video qualified that blunt statement by saying that members of the media "don't wish for the deaths of innocent people," but then it said, "The truth of the matter is that if there is one organization in this country that has a vested interest in the perpetuation of mass tragedy, it is our mainstream media."

That is, quite simply, a dreadful thing to say. How do you start a conversation with someone who tells you that you "love mass shootings"?

While I don't live in New York or D.C., I do interact with quite a few members of the mainstream media—from cable hosts to producers to print reporters—and I can assure you that this sentiment is every bit as slanderous to their characters as the claim that gun rights supporters "don't care" when kids are gunned down in schools. Yes, media organizations get higher ratings after mass killings. Yes, their anti-gun arguments have a higher profile. But the same thing is true on the other side. Gun rights organizations get more clicks, they raise more money, and their arguments gain a higher profile after events like Parkland.

Does that mean they love mass shootings? Of course not.

My former *National Review* colleague Kevin Williamson has long argued that the gun control debate isn't a matter of policy but of *Kulturkampf*. The mutual disdain isn't limited to vigorous disagreement about background checks; it extends to a perceived way of life. As Williamson observes, some progressives believe that firearms are little more than "an atavistic enthusiasm for rural primitives and right-wing militia nuts, a hobby that must be tolerated—if only barely—because of some vestigial 18th-century political compromise."[6] They simply do not grasp—or care to grasp—how "gun culture" is truly lived in red America.

This is the mindset that exists after the Overton window has moved so far to the left as to preclude consideration of conservative views.

This loathing isn't one-sided. It's simply false to believe that the haters are clustered on the left side of the spectrum and the right is plaintively seeking greater understanding. Increasingly, conservatives don't just hate their liberal counterparts; they despise the perceived culture of blue America. They're repulsed by the notion that personal security should depend almost completely on the government. The sense of dependence is at odds with their view of a free citizenry, and—to put it bluntly—they perceive their progressive fellow citizens as soft and unmanly.

This is what happens when the Overton window moves so far to the right that it precludes even basic respect for the people who seek to change your mind.

And unlike the astounding Twitter hysterics over net neutrality, tax policy, or regulatory reform, the gun debate really is—at its heart—about life and death. It's about different ways of life, different ways of perceiving your role in a nation and a community.

It's long been the case that the more important the issue, the greater the difficulty in discussing it civilly and respectfully. Emotions run high even in the best of times. The old admonition against discussing religion and politics at the dinner table is rooted in this long-standing truth. But there is a vast difference between a difficult conversation and an exchange of verbal fire. There is a vast difference between disagreeing with your opponent and believing their views are outside the realm of acceptable discourse.

And if you believe your opponent's views are outside the realm of acceptable discourse, it's a very short trip to conclude that they shouldn't enjoy the right to speak at all.

Losing the Free Speech Culture

O ne of my favorite people in all of the United States is my liberal civil libertarian friend Greg Lukianoff. Greg is the president of the Foundation for Individual Rights in Education (FIRE), one of the last truly non-partisan civil liberties organizations in the United States. Founded by University of Pennsylvania history professor Alan Charles Kors and former ACLU attorney Harvey Silverglate, it defends individual liberty in higher education—regardless of your ideology. It doesn't matter if you're a home-schooled primitive Baptist or a lesbian vegan pagan, FIRE protects your rights (full disclosure: I was president of FIRE in 2004 and 2005, and Greg worked with me as FIRE's legal director).

Greg has been doing this for so long—and he's seen so many cases—that it's fair to say that when he speaks about liberty, it's time to listen. He has been at the cutting edge of a civil libertarian movement that has noticed a disturbing change particularly in youth attitudes toward free speech. As Greg's former colleague at FIRE and a free speech attorney for a quarter century, I've filed more than my share of cases combating campus censorship. As a general rule, those cases have involved top-down punishment of typically Christian or conservative students or student groups who violated campus speech codes or "diversity" policies. A small cohort of radical progressive administrators, usually deans or student life administrators, took the lead in suppressing speech, and the student body—to the extent it had an opinion at all—was generally hostile to censorship.

There were exceptions, of course, but for twenty years the pattern held. Then, as Greg noted in an influential cover story in *The Atlantic* (co-authored with New York University social psychologist Jonathan Haidt), "something strange" started happening. A movement arose, "undirected and driven largely by students, to scrub campuses clean of words, ideas, and subjects that might cause discomfort or give offense."[1] The key phrase was "driven largely by students." Censorship was now a grassroots effort.

The examples Greg used were largely classic cases of political correctness—but political correctness pushed from the bottom up, not the top down. At Harvard Law School, students asked their professors not to teach the criminal law legal doctrines regarding rape and sexual assault. At Northwestern University, a professor named Laura Kipnis was subjected to student Title IX complaints because she wrote an article for the *Chronicle of Higher Education*, the nation's leading magazine focused on university life, arguing that Title IX regulations had gone too far and that a professor on campus had been subjected to an unfair investigation. The students were so offended by her argument, they considered it a civil rights violation.

A sense of fear was so pervasive that in June 2015, a professor wrote an anonymous piece on *Vox* that was titled "I'm a Liberal Professor, and My Liberal Students Terrify Me."

And that was before a wave of violence hit college campuses. In November 2015, aggressive activism at the University of Missouri culminated in efforts to block the media from covering student protests and featured a viral video of a professor, Melissa Click, caught on camera calling for student "muscle" to clear out a student journalist.

In early 2016, students at California State University in Los Angeles used violence and threats of violence to try to block access to a speech by conservative writer and podcaster Ben Shapiro. From there, the problem spiraled out of control. In February 2017, rioters blocked a speech at the University of California, Berkeley, by former Breitbart writer (and alt-right apologist) Milo Yiannopoulos. In March, a mob at Colby College shouted down American Enterprise Institute scholar Charles Murray and attacked him as he tried to leave campus, injuring a professor.

The list could go on. One of the ugliest incidents occurred at Evergreen State College, where professor Bret Weinstein faced threats after he objected to a planned protest that asked white faculty, students, and staff to leave campus for a day. Weinstein, an avowed progressive, believed the protest was counterproductive, and his comments immediately provoked a menacing backlash. And he wasn't alone. Video raced across the internet of students trapping Evergreen administrators in rooms, preventing them from leaving even to go to the bathroom.

By mid-2017 (dubbed "the year of the shout-down" by the Center for Ethics in Public Policy's Stanley Kurtz), violent or intimidating incidents on campus were so common that many of them barely made the news.[2] In September of

that year, only a massive police presence could guarantee
Ben Shapiro's safety at a UC Berkeley speech. Police arrested nine people—four for carrying banned weapons.[3]
What was happening? The answer is complex. Indeed,
one could write an entire book exploring the reasons
for the grassroots violence and censorship. And, in fact,
that's exactly what Lukianoff and Haidt did, publishing
2018's *The Coddling of the American Mind*.

Lukianoff and Haidt decry "safetyism," a parental
philosophy—often deployed by upper-middle-class "helicopter parents"—that places safety and comfort over
adventure and exploration. Safetyism encourages students to think of themselves as fragile and to demand
that institutions provide them with spaces of emotional
and physical comfort. At the extremes, students now even
think of speech as "violence," justifying a physical response
in sheer self-defense.

Critics of Lukianoff and Haidt accused them of "ca-
tastrophizing" the problem—of taking isolated, extreme
events and categorizing them as typical of the college
experience. But that's wrong. There's considerable data
to suggest that there is rising cultural hostility to free
speech. Simply put, while students will pay lip service to
free speech, a shockingly high percentage support censorship and shout-downs to block speech they dislike.

For example, in October 2017, Yale's William F. Buck-
ley Program released the results of a survey showing that
while strong majorities proclaim support for free speech,
that support collapses the instant they're asked to defend
expression they find offensive.[4] A full 58 percent of students believe that colleges should "forbid" speakers who
have a "history of engaging in hate speech." And what is

hate speech? The definition the students liked was staggeringly broad. Two-thirds agreed that hate speech is "anything that one particular person believes is harmful, racist, or bigoted." They further agreed that hate speech "means something different to everyone." Even worse, 81 percent of the surveyed students agreed with the statement that "words can be a form of violence."

Given these realities, it should come as no surprise that large numbers of students believed that interruptions and sometimes violence are appropriate to stop offensive speech. Almost 40 percent believed that it's "sometimes appropriate" to "shout down or disrupt" a speaker. A sobering 30 percent believed that physical violence may be used to stop someone from "using hate speech or engaging in racially charged comments."

Sure, that's one survey, but others show similarly disturbing results. A 2017 Brookings Institution survey showed that a slight majority of students (including 62 percent of Democrats) believed it was appropriate to disrupt and shout down a speaker "known for making offensive and hurtful" comments.[5] A troubling 19 percent (including 20 percent of Democrats and 22 percent of Republicans) believed it was acceptable to use violence to prevent the speaker from giving his or her speech.

A majority of students believed it was preferable for a university to "create a positive learning environment for all students by prohibiting certain speech or expression of viewpoints that are offensive or biased against certain groups of people." They preferred censorship to the alternative vision, a university that "create[s] an open learning environment where students are exposed to all types of speech and viewpoints, even if it means allowing speech that is offensive or biased against certain groups of people."

Sure, that's two surveys, but is there a third? Indeed there is. In March 2018, Gallup and the Knight Foundation released the results of a new survey of 3,014 college students.[6] On the one hand, its results were sadly familiar. An overwhelming majority (89 percent) said it was "extremely" or "very" important to protect citizens' free-speech rights, but a full 64 percent said the First Amendment shouldn't protect so-called hate speech. A strong majority (60 percent) supported restricting even costumes that "stereotype certain racial or ethnic groups." Almost half of students supported establishing speech codes, and 61 percent said the "climate on my campus prevents some people from saying things they believe because others might find them offensive."

But hidden elsewhere within the poll was perhaps the key question of the free-speech debate, a question that starkly illustrates exactly how free-speech controversies are framed and how students process the "cost" of the First Amendment. When asked to choose between free speech and inclusivity, the students chose inclusivity by a 53–46 percent margin.

When I first read the survey, I objected to the question. We are not "forced to choose" between inclusivity and free speech. But upon reflection, I realized the question's worth. That's exactly how free-speech debates are framed on campus. That's exactly how free-speech debates are increasingly framed off campus, especially in the ideological monoculture of Silicon Valley. Advocates of free speech are often cast as enemies of diversity and opponents of inclusion. Students are told time and again that if they value historically marginalized communities, then they should endeavor to protect them from problematic or offensive speech.

Now, let's think of the application of these surveys—of this grassroots censorship—to the Overton window. Increasingly, if a conservative wishes to dialogue with progressives, especially but not exclusively on campus, then there is a chance not only that campus radicals will refuse to hear the debate, but that many of them will actively try to block the debate from happening.

It's a surreal experience to prepare for a college presentation on the First Amendment and have to sit for a security briefing by the chief of campus police. It's surreal to be taught escape routes and to have a police officer shadow you before and after you speak. It's surreal, but it's a new normal when you want to argue, say, for conventional constitutional concepts like religious liberty or freedom of expression.

Moreover, it's important to pause for a moment and ponder how wrong it is to put free speech and inclusion at odds. No one is more empowered by free speech than the historically marginalized and dispossessed. I'll repeat Frederick Douglass's declaration from 1860: free speech is the "great moral renovator of society and government." He argued that "slavery cannot tolerate free speech" and that "five years of its exercise would banish the auction block and break every chain in the South."[7]

The antebellum South did indeed crack down on free speech. In fact, the First Amendment would not explicitly apply to the states until the Supreme Court's 1925

decision in *Gitlow v. New York*. Thus, throughout slavery
and for much of the Jim Crow era, black Americans were
helpless in the face of *state* government suppression of
free speech, as numerous American states implemented
regimes that tyrannized their African American citizens.

During the civil rights era, federal court rulings defeating state efforts to suppress the civil rights movement
were ultimately indispensable to the cause of equality. I
remember once asking the Reverend Walter Fauntroy, an
early member of the Congressional Black Caucus, why
he believed the movement for African American equality made such rapid legal gains once it was able to fully
mobilize. "Almighty God and the First Amendment," he
responded. The First Amendment gave the most visible
marginalized group in American history a voice, and
God softened people's hearts to hear the message that
spread as a result.

The true tension in the First Amendment isn't between freedom and diversity or freedom and inclusion.
History teaches us that the tension is between freedom
and power. Free speech, by its very nature, leads to questioning, debate, and—eventually—accountability.

In reality, speech is the engine that powers American diversity. Individual liberty is indispensable to true
inclusivity. Thus, it's incompatible with the incomplete
diversity that's often advanced on the college campus,
which celebrates differences in sexuality and ethnicity
but increasingly expects its faculty and students to think
alike. And it's incompatible with the false inclusivity of
the modern university, which all too often excludes even
the most credible and serious voices if those voices challenge the orthodoxies of identity politics.

Our students "unlearn liberty"—to borrow Lukia-noff's excellent phrase—in part because they've been presented with a false choice. The true conflict isn't between speech and diversity, it's between speech and the unaccountable power that political and cultural leaders so consistently crave.

Losing a Common Political Language

C ompeting Overton windows drive hostility, they drive censorship, and they also drive incomprehension. Especially at the ideological edges—among the people most committed to political and cultural change—it often seems as if we no longer speak the same language. Even the most basic words don't have the same meaning in different political communities.

Take, for example, the word "racism."

By 2018, the intolerance of the college campus was migrating fully into pop culture and mass media. Hostile Twitter personalities on the left and right combed through Twitter profiles and reread old columns in the effort to find something, anything, so offensive that it could torpedo a career or lead to a vitriolic public shaming. My friend and colleague Kevin Williamson was hired—then fired—at *The Atlantic* after an old podcast segment surfaced in which he seemed to advocate the death penalty for women who have abortions. In reality, he's a death penalty opponent. He was doing what writers often do, conducting a thought experiment to test principles.

The *New York Times* hired writer Quinn Norton, then

fired her—within *hours*—after controversial tweets surfaced where she used anti-gay slurs and retweeted a racist term. It's not that anyone actually thought she was a homophobe or a bigot, and the tweets were explainable in context, but the firestorm was just too much for the *Times.*

So it was extremely interesting when the *Times* hired Asian American journalist Sarah Jeong and then stood behind her when her controversial tweets surfaced. And those tweets were indeed controversial.[1] In them, Jeong expressed some rather interesting views of "dumba[**] f[***]ing white people," musing about how much joy she gets "out of being cruel to old white men" and how "white men are bullsh[**]." For good measure she also compared white people to "groveling goblins" and wondered whether they're "genetically predisposed to burn faster in the sun."

Jeong explained the tweets as "counter-trolling" designed to mimic the language of racists who targeted her online, but that explanation made little sense in context. Many of her most offensive tweets seemed spontaneous. They weren't made in response to any identifiable provocation. They instead seemed—from context—to express her sincere feelings about white people.

Conservatives were incredulous. Why the double standard? If any white writer had said similar things about any other racial group, they'd have been fired immediately. Was the argument that some forms of racism were more acceptable than others?

No, that wasn't the argument. Instead, legions of progressives took to Twitter to explain that conservatives didn't understand what racism actually was. For example, *Vox* writer Zack Beauchamp tweeted that "A lot of people on the internet today [are] confusing the expressive way anti-racists and minorities talk about 'white people' with actual race-based hatred, for some unfathomable reason."

Bloomberg's David Joachim tweeted, "Dear white people: 1. Racism is [about] the powerful keeping down the powerless; 2. We (generally) are the powerful; 3. 'White ppl' isn't a slur; 4. 'Fag' and the N word are slurs, because they subordinate; 5. Your moral equivalence is nonsense; 6. 'Reverse racism' isn't a thing."

These comments echo ideas that have gained increasing currency in progressive circles. Essentially, they're tied to the notion that anti-white rhetoric and ideas can't be "racism" because either such rhetoric is justified or it's not connected to power. In other words, racism doesn't simply mean "hatred for a person because of his or her race." It means hatred *by the powerful against the powerless* on the basis of race.

But this isn't a common definition. It's a left-wing definition that's gained traction within the left-wing Overton window. It's mystifying to conservatives who live largely outside of progressive communities.

There are ways through these windows into actual conversation, but you have to know the competing terms of the debate. Unless you do, then the two sides are simply ships passing in the night. I'm reminded of lyrics from "The Sound of Silence," the Simon and Garfunkel classic: "People talking without speaking. People hearing without listening."

So, in response to the Jeong controversy, I tried to acknowledge this different definition of racism and respond. I argued that the new definition of racism confused the *gravity* of an offense with the *existence* of the offense. A powerless person's hate may not harm the powerful, but it is still hate. A powerless person's hate may even be grounded in specific experiences, but it is still hate. The essence of bigotry is to look at the color of a person's skin and, on that basis alone, make malicious judgments about their character or worth.

Moreover, I argued, it is simply false to excuse anti-white racism on the grounds that people of color lack power. There are certainly many millions of vulnerable and marginalized individuals in this nation, and they are disproportionately (though not entirely) black and brown. But when anti-white sentiment is embedded in the *New York Times* editorial board, it's no longer "powerless" in any meaningful sense. Similarly, when it reaches the heights of government, the academy, or the bestseller lists, it's no longer remotely "powerless."

That's not an argument that power doesn't matter. Of course it does. Power matters. And so does purpose. That's why no one should compare Jeong's comments to the racism you see on racist websites like Stormfront or to the deadly racism in Charlottesville that horrified the nation in 2017.

Racism married to violence or violent intent is categorically different from the anti-white racism you see in certain quarters of the elite identity-politics left. Similarly, racism married to state policies—especially state policies of the relatively recent American past, which continue to have malignant effects on poor and disadvantaged Americans—is categorically different from the anti-white racism that exists in parts of the academy or in segments of American media.

The threat of anti-white racism isn't violence (except

in rare cases). It's not systematic oppression. There's no realistic scenario where "the tables are turned" and black Americans visit on white Americans a reverse version of the worst aspects of American history. The problem with anti-white racism is that it runs directly counter to efforts to unify in spite of that history. It runs counter to efforts to elevate American culture. And, yes, it can and does create individual injustice in those instances where anti-white racism manifests itself in more than just tweets and academic articles.

Finally, to indulge at all the notion that injustice, even systematic injustice, can excuse or legitimize hatred against a class or group of Americans is to open Pandora's box. I've seen it argued across the breadth of the Web that anti-white sentiment is a legitimate and understandable response to the actions of white people and "white" power structures.

Veterans of our Middle Eastern wars have seen jihadist horrors on a scale that most Americans can't comprehend. Is it a legitimate response for a veteran to go on a Twitter screed about "canceling" Arabs or to compare them to "groveling goblins" (as Jeong did to white people)? Should a white victim of a black criminal draw conclusions about black people more generally? Even if they can point to disproportionate levels of violent crime?

Of course not.

A healthy society urges people to reject unhealthy temptations to generalize, and instead urges that we treat our fellow citizens with a degree of grace and to judge them based on their individual actions. Any categorical hatred or disgust stands directly against this virtue. So, yes, anti-white racism is real, and Americans can and should reject it while still keeping in mind matters of gravity and proportion.

Share these sentiments with people outside of America's activist class, and they strike people as extremely basic, perhaps nothing more than an expression of common sense. *Of course* judging people on the basis of skin color is wrong. *Of course* we can differentiate between the historical experiences of different American groups.

But one of the lessons of the modern era is that while you can try to understand the other side and engage in good faith, the real energy is on the side of scorn and shame. The people who care the most about politics, who drive the day-to-day national conversation, give no quarter to opponents. They condemn any effort at moderation and believe that the very effort to see whether there is merit in an opposing view necessitates dangerous compromise and accommodation.

Thus, to some, the only thing that mattered about my response to the Jeong controversy was my race. I was just another white man, "so blissfully protected by the currency of Whiteness, that [I'm] simply not capable of removing the veil of ignorance."[2] Thus there is no conversation. The righteous speak. The sinners listen.

I bring up this tempest not because it was particularly important on its own, but because it's representative. Versions of this "argument" play out every week and every month of every modern year, and each time the opposing activists grow angrier. They grow more convinced not just of the righteousness of their cause, but also of the perfidy of their opposition.

And what of the people who seek to navigate the competing arguments to find the messy and complicated truth? Often they stay silent. They see what happens to those who question one or both of the competing activist narratives about American life. They watch the online gang-tackles and say to themselves, "It's not worth it." They concede the marketplace of ideas to the loudest and angriest Americans.

In this environment, "free speech" isn't about dialogue. It's about transmitting truth to the unenlightened. It's an exercise of power. For angry activists, speech is a sword. Censorship and shame campaigns are a shield. Activists wield the sword to slice and dice opponents, and wield the shield to protect themselves from the pain of disagreement, or —heaven forbid—the wrenching pain of being exposed as wrong or misguided.

The goal is domination, not discussion, and certainly not coexistence. "The only way is through," remember? The only way is to "reorder" the public square. It's time to impose the "common good" or the "Highest Good." The instrument is power. Resistance is evidence of depravity.

In reality, however, the very act of attempting to use the levers of political and economic power to drive your opponent to the edges of American influence inflames every single flash point of division articulated in this book. It breaks the fundamental compact between citizen and state. And if that political power is brought to bear clumsily or maliciously in a time of national upheaval, then the results could be catastrophic. The nation could fracture.

How? Let's roll the trends of geographic separation, group polarization, and illiberal intolerance forward to an all-too-foreseeable future. It's time to explore how the ultimate national tragedy could occur. It's time to ponder two potential scenarios for secession.

PART II

The Dissolution

Calexit

It was possibly the most savage and cruel mass shooting in American history. On the anniversary of the April 20, 1999, Columbine High School massacre, two young men, wearing trench coats and armed to the teeth with semiautomatic rifles and pistols, walked into a California high school and opened fire. Their attack represented the third mass school shooting since September, and already the fifth large-scale mass shooting in the state in the calendar year.

But what made this particular attack so heinous wasn't just the target—and it wasn't even the weapons. It was the tactics. One of the men dedicated himself to murder in the classrooms while the other held off the police as long as he could, peppering the parking lot with gunfire as officers raced to respond, pinning them down behind squad cars as they frantically sought alternative ways to enter the building.

By the time the smoke cleared, thirty-five kids lay dead. Two cops sacrificed their lives, and five more suffered grave injuries.

The nation was shocked. The community mourned. California, however, reacted with white-hot rage. Already the state had the most restrictive gun control the law would allow. It imposed universal background checks, including on ammunition purchases, but the Supreme Court had struck down most of the state's efforts to restrict firearms. Five years before the massacre the Court had overturned California's ban on assault weapons and large-capacity magazines by a 5–4 vote, a decision that triggered waves of protest in cities across the state.

Moreover, by a 6–3 vote in the Court, California was now a "shall issue" concealed-carry state, granting citizens the right to carry firearms if they could pass a background check. And when the shooting happened the Supreme Court was considering whether to grant review in a case challenging the state's ten-day waiting period for most firearm purchases.

And what kinds of weapons did the shooters use? Semiautomatic rifles with thirty-round magazines and semiautomatic pistols with fifteen-round magazines— legally purchased not long after the Supreme Court rulings. In public protests and in online debates, people in California accused the conservative justices of the Supreme Court of murdering their children. They accused the Court of overriding their right to self-government and placing their lives at risk—all to placate a president and a party bought and sold by the gun lobby.

Not only had the Supreme Court, they claimed, put their lives in danger by putting more weapons on the streets, but the Court's rhetoric (which had waxed eloquent about the historic role of the firearm in the American culture of self-defense and self-governance) had—according to angry Californians—"inspired" the killers.

By this point, gun ownership in the state had dwindled

considerably. Geographic sorting and group polarization had rendered gun ownership a cultural anathema in most large California communities. Gun owners represented a small and insignificant California constituency. Millions of Californians didn't know anyone who owned a gun, and they couldn't imagine a rational argument for having a weapon in their home, much less on their person.

The community of gun owners was thoroughly marginalized. Gun owners generally lived well outside urban city centers, and even there they were often subject to online shame campaigns if they posted pictures of their firearms or pictures of themselves hunting with friends and family.

Thus, when the legislature acted in response to the shooting, there was no meaningful opposition. There were few voices in the room to moderate the debate or moderate the emotion of the moment. Instead, the legislature radicalized. Moving with remarkable speed, it passed the Save Our Lives Act, banning private ownership of most classes of firearms and imposing a mandatory gun buyback program on all California citizens. Visitors to California from other states were flatly banned from bringing any weapons into the state, even for hunting, and Hollywood's firearms were seized, catalogued, and placed under state control—to be dispensed only during filming and observed throughout by the state's newly created "gun marshals."

The legislature knew it had defied Supreme Court precedent when it voted to send the bill to the governor's desk. The governor knew she defied Supreme Court precedent when she signed it. Yet the bill contained no grace period. There was no grandfathering. Gun buybacks were to begin immediately, and a tip line was established for citizens to report neighbors who they believed owned guns. The state established a website for citizens to forward social media posts purporting to show gun ownership. Failure to surrender weapons for buyback carried a substantial criminal penalty—up to five years in prison and a fine of no less than $5,000.

The instant the law went into effect, a coalition of gun owners—acting anonymously as "John Does" to avoid gun confiscation—filed a request for a temporary restraining order to block enforcement of the new law. The judge, who had been appointed by the most recent Democratic president, refused. And so did a three-judge panel of the Ninth Circuit Court of Appeals that, days later, heard the gun owners' emergency appeal.

Each court made similar arguments: that the Second Amendment properly understood protected merely the individual right to join a state-organized militia, and with the rise of the National Guard the Second Amendment no longer had meaningful application to modern American life. The Supreme Court had long rejected this interpretation of the Second Amendment, but it did not matter. Progressive justices were drawing a line in the sand and daring the high court to overrule them, again.

As the plaintiffs raced to prepare their papers for their petition to the Supreme Court, state officials began enforcing the law. In fact, they'd begun enforcing the law the moment it was enacted. Relying on neighbors' tips and old social media posts, law enforcement fanned out across rural towns and neighborhoods. While few people voluntarily turned in their weapons, most people peacefully (but grudgingly) handed over their guns when confronted by police. In multiple locations, however, angry confrontations turned into actual firefights, and by week's end two gun owners were dead and three law enforcement officers were gravely hurt. In one terrible case, a child was caught in the crossfire and died in her own home when her father refused to surrender his handgun. Tragically and provocatively, he had posted a picture of that same gun on social media just that very morning, with the caption *"molon labe"*—ancient Greek for "come and take it." Police came. They took his gun. They also took his daughter's life.

As the nation's eyes were fixed on California, multiple militia groups from the "red West"—states like Montana, Idaho, and the Dakotas—vowed to mobilize to come to the aid of gun owners in California's rural regions. The threat was more boast than promise, but as small groups of armed men gathered together and posted pictures online, California residents reacted with renewed fury. Immense crowds gathered in Sacramento, San Francisco, and Los Angeles demanding that the governor "defend California."

Responding to the threat, the governor ordered checkpoints established at the state border on roads into California and ordered the highway patrol to search "suspicious" vehicles entering the state. Traffic backed up on the California border for miles, and yet another round of lawsuits started rocketing through the federal courts—this time seeking the freedom to travel freely across state lines.

The president of the United States was taken by surprise by the crisis. He had attended a memorial service in Sacramento two days after the shooting, but he left for the airport directly after the eulogy. Like most GOP officeholders, he always kept his visits to California brief. The Republican Party in the state was weak, and every trip featured loud and angry protests. Besides, he was a strong supporter of Second Amendment rights, and he knew the protests would be particularly vociferous. He did his duty by attending the funeral. He met with the family members who would meet with him, and then he took off—leaving without meeting with a coalition of Democratic officeholders who had demanded that the president host a national gun control town hall.

The president had won his first election the classic Republican way—holding all the Southeast and Midwest strongholds while winning Minnesota and Pennsylvania, two of the last remaining true swing states in the United States. He then won reelection in a contentious, vicious campaign marked by street demonstrations, particularly heated negative campaigning, and claims of voter suppression.

To make matters worse, he lost the popular vote in his reelection campaign by more than 2 million votes, the third Republican in modern times to win the White House with a minority of the popular vote. Millions of Americans (including millions of Californians) not only believed their president was a heartless, racist, violent radical, but also believed he was fundamentally illegitimate. He was evidence of the failure of American democracy.

Consequently, in spite of the fact that the president was "squeaky clean" (as was his Democratic opponent—the parties had learned valuable lessons about the dangers of running corrupt candidates), a near-record number of Americans viewed him "very unfavorably." At the same time, he was a virtual hero to much of red America. A near-record number viewed him "very favorably," and some of his political rallies drew crowds so large that he'd long ago stopped giving speeches in small venues like basketball arenas. In the states of the Deep South, he could fill a football stadium.

But he could barely fill a high school gymnasium in California, especially in urban California. He'd lost the state by 35 points and more than 5 million votes. When Air Force One flew into Sacramento, the airport was besieged by protesters. His motorcade slowed to a crawl in the effort to reach the memorial service, and some protesters got close enough to bang on the windows of his vehicle. The images were broadcast live across the United States, and his voters in red states reacted in disgust.

The "California mob," as the president's supporters put it, was at it again. After all, this wasn't the first time that the rest of America had watched large-scale defiance on the West Coast. The previous year's "sanctuary movement" (critics called it the "sanctuary siege") was credited with galvanizing resistance to the president in California *and* with galvanizing the president's base.

California's expanding sanctuary state laws (ironically enough, upheld by the same Supreme Court that its residents now vilified) had blocked state authorities from offering any assistance to federal officials enforcing national immigration laws. Yet as the Republican administration flooded the state with new federal agents to compensate for lack of access to state assets, California activists responded. For a period of three months, a rotating cast of thousands surrounded federal facilities in the state. They blocked roads, pitched tents on helipads, and presented federal authorities with a choice: stop immigration enforcement in the interior of the state or confront the protesters.

The administration chose confrontation. In one dramatic week, federal officials moved aggressively to arrest and clear the encampments. The resulting confrontations were described as "mostly peaceful" by the progressive press and "violent" by the conservative media. Yes, most protesters engaged in classic civil disobedience—allowing themselves to be arrested and transported off-site without violent resistance—but some used more aggressive tactics. In some cases, the streets filled with tear gas, federal officials used stun guns, and in two separate incidents clashes escalated to deadly force. When federal forces finally broke the sieges, forty federal officers were treated for mostly minor wounds, more than five hundred protesters were transported to hospitals, and two young men died.

In the end, both sides were furious. Californians hated the crackdown, and immigration officials—though able to perform their jobs—faced daily harassment. Federal offices occasionally faced renewed sieges that could last for hours and days at a time.

Red Americans were aghast at the lawlessness. Talking heads chattered about a "nullification crisis," and the angriest voices urged the deployment of troops. They called the sanctuary sieges a "violent insurrection." They compared it to the Whiskey Rebellion, Shays's Rebellion, and other popular uprisings, and they demanded an even stronger federal response. "It's not just about California," they said. After all, immigrants living in California could freely cross state lines and flood neighboring states with illegal entrants. In response, the "red West" sent a surge of law enforcement assets to border roads. Traffic stops increased, and cries of "racial profiling" filled the air.

And so when California began its gun crackdown, the president had precious few cards to play. He had been taken by surprise by the speed with which the Save Our Lives Act had moved through the legislature. He was further taken by surprise by the speed at which California had moved to enforce the law. And now he was alarmed at the violence. But so far federal courts had upheld California's law, and he feared that if he moved decisively before the Supreme Court ruled, he'd trigger large-scale, violent resistance.

Empowered by the lower courts, California officials stepped up their confiscation program. There were now more than twenty thousand state law enforcement officials actively engaged in gun collection efforts. They had fanned out across the state, and in numerous places were surrounding the homes of defiant gun owners.

In the meantime, the California governor was enjoying a massive surge in popularity. Across left-wing social media she was lionized as the woman who finally defeated the NRA. Think pieces hailed her "defense of the true meaning of the Second Amendment," and even the tactics of the crackdown. The sheer speed of California's actions, they noted, prevented scattered California gun owners from organizing a violent resistance, caught the hated Republican government in Washington flat-footed, and kept even the crazed militias from responding in an organized fashion.

Never mind that the crackdown had netted a relatively small percentage of the millions of guns still in private hands in the state; the perception of effectiveness was overwhelming, and palpable despair gripped the remaining California gun owners. They were alone. The president refused to act. All their hopes rested with the Supreme Court, but if it ruled in their favor, who would enforce its order?

Oral arguments were held on a beautiful spring day in Washington. Protesters on both sides virtually blanketed the Supreme Court building. They were separated by a phalanx of police. Longtime Supreme Court reporters described the atmosphere inside the building as "icy cold." None of the normal collegiality was present. The three justices of the Court's liberal wing barely glanced at their colleagues. The chief justice looked stricken.

The plaintiffs' attorney—the lawyer representing the anonymous California gun owners—stood to speak first. He was immediately interrupted. "What, pray tell, do your clients need with an assault rifle and a thirty-round magazine? Do they need a weapon like that to defend their house? Do they need a weapon like that to hunt deer? Or are your clients interested in hunting people?"

Another justice interjected: "Prior precedents have accepted that Americans enjoy a right of self-defense. They have not accepted that Americans enjoy a right of self-defense with the weapon of their choice. How many innocent people have to die before you understand or recognize that there is a compelling state interest in limiting the ability of a deranged man to commit mass slaughter?"

The first justice spoke again. "Counsel, how many mass shootings have been committed with revolvers in the last decade? Do you know?"

There was a pause for just a moment as the attorney for the John Does waited to see if another question or comment was incoming. "The record of this case does not contain a complete study of weapons used in all mass shoot—"

One of the justices interrupted him. "Let me help you there. I did my own study and determined that there was not a single mass shooting—not one—committed by shooters using the weapons still permissible under California law. There was not one mass shooting committed with a revolver. There was not one mass shooting committed with the types of shotguns still permitted. And do you know what else we found?"

"No, I do not."

"We found hundreds—no, thousands—of examples of lawful self-defense with revolvers. We found many incidents of lawful home defense with a shotgun. Are you telling me that your clients are so inept that they can't defend their homes with a pump-action shotgun?"

The attorney paused for a moment and waited to see if another question was coming. Then he responded.

"But that's not the analysis. By stripping my law-abiding clients of their weapons, you don't actually remove semiautomatic pistols or semiautomatic rifles from the population. You just remove them from the law-abiding population, leaving my clients at a serious disadvantage in any confrontation with the criminal class. If a revolver and pump-action shotgun were sufficient to keep the peace, why do police still roll throughout California with Glocks and AR-15s?

"Moreover," he continued, "as I'm sure your research found, so-called assault weapons account for only the tiniest fraction of murders in California—legal revolvers cause more deaths—and gun owners have in multiple cases used AR-15s to defend their lives and their homes."

That was the plaintiffs' counsel's longest statement of the oral argument. The justices largely ignored the plaintiffs' lawyer and began arguing sharply among themselves. The bickering became so pronounced that the chief justice at one point slammed his hand down on the bench to restore order.

And, make no mistake, the attorney general of California fared little better when he stood to make his argument. The only surprise was the justice who spoke up first—the quiet conservative, the justice who rarely uttered a syllable at oral arguments. He cross-examined the attorney general, asking rapid-fire questions that gave no opportunity for another justice to interject.

"You are aware of this court's precedents in *Heller*, *McDonald*, *Gomez*, and *Hanson*, are you not?"

"Yes, but—"

"Just yes will suffice. You are aware that those precedents have not been overturned, correct?"

"Yes, but—"

"Again, I need nothing but a yes here. And each member of your legislature and your governor were aware of those precedents when they drafted and signed this legislation, were they not?"

"Yes."

"Are you familiar with pre–Civil War arguments about nullification?"

"Yes."

"Do you believe your state has the constitutional power to nullify a precedent from this Court?"

"May I respond?"

"You may."

"Our position is that our sovereign state has the right and responsibility to protect its citizens and to uphold the constitution of the state, and the Constitution of these United States. It is our belief that present Supreme Court precedent regarding the Second Amendment is as flawed as cases like *Korematsu* and *Dred Scott*—cases that we're rightly ashamed of today. Each court below has agreed with our assessment of the law, and now we are asking this Court to conform its precedent to the original meaning of the Constitution and to restore to our state the sovereign respect it is due under our federal system."

The "quiet" conservative justice responded: "You argue that your brief and your position support the original meaning of the Constitution, yet that's an assertion devoid of support. It's devoid of meaningful historical scholarship. It's devoid of any historical frame of reference. You assert this as a talking point, as a position for the cameras, not as a legal position that any thinking judge"—he glanced meaningfully at his more liberal colleagues—"would accept as a properly supported legal argument. The Framers unquestionably intended for private citizens to possess military-grade weapons, not just as a form of protection against crime but as a last line of defense against a tyrannical state, a use that some of those weapons are being put to now."

"You're not suggesting—"

"I am suggesting that your state government is grotesquely, intentionally, and now violently violating the clearly established constitutional rights of its citizens. *That* is what I am suggesting. That is all that I am suggesting."

And with that he slumped back in his chair, a scowl on his face.

The decision was a foregone conclusion. California lost. The only surprise was the margin. Rather than the expected 6–3, it was 5–4. Five justices ruled unequivocally and in the strongest judicial language that California had violated the Second Amendment. Three justices ruled unequivocally and in the strongest judicial language that California's law was consistent with a proper reading of the Second Amendment. One justice—the chief justice—wrote an impassioned dissent reconsidering the entire doctrine of incorporation, the legal doctrine that applied the provisions of the Bill of Rights to state governments. He sensed the magnitude of the American divide and sought a constitutional method for restoring federalism—by reinterpreting the Fourteenth Amendment narrowly and state sovereignty broadly.

The Second Amendment, he argued, should restrain the federal government only, not the state government, and if California wanted to establish itself as America's largest gun-free zone—just as it had established itself as America's largest sanctuary state—it should indeed be permitted to do so.

Ironically, the chief justice's plea for accommodation only magnified the national split. Once again, a monumental case was decided by a 5–4 margin. This 5–4 margin existed against the backdrop of *two* instances in which a GOP-controlled Senate had blocked a Democratic president's Supreme Court appointment without a hearing, the second time leading to an astounding twenty-three-month vacancy before the election of the current president.

On the morning the Supreme Court announced its opinion, three momentous things happened at once. First, as expected, California citizens protested by the hundreds of thousands. Every federal law enforcement office in the state once again found itself under siege. Anticipating the Court's decision, federal law enforcement buildings had been emptied of all workers except those necessary to establish site security, but aside from those who could do paperwork from home, federal law enforcement essentially ceased to function in the state of California.

Second, the governor of California announced that while she would not resist enforcement of the Supreme Court's order, she would not enforce it. In other words, she directed state agencies to continue enforcement of the Save Our Lives Act unless and until directed in person to stop by a federal law enforcement official possessing a written court order. But since federal law enforcement was under siege, California police were able to continue their work unmolested.

Third, and perhaps most consequentially, the commander of the California National Guard sent a confidential message to the Pentagon indicating that he believed the Posse Comitatus Act prohibited him from taking any

action to enforce the Court's order, and—furthermore—
even if he received lawful federal instructions to enforce
the Court's ruling, he would decline to do so, indicating
that he could not be certain of his soldiers' willingness to
confront California law enforcement. After all, like many
state national guards, his ranks included a number of civilian law enforcement officials who maintained parallel
military careers. They would not detain, much less train
their guns on, the men and women who worked beside
them in their civilian lives.

At this point, it was clear that the president faced an
actual insurrection. It was still largely peaceful, but it
was quite clear that California was defying federal authority, and it was winning.

And so fury built on the right.

With each new arrest, with each new police siege,
and with each small-scale firefight, the president's base
clamored for action. They demanded federal intervention.
Within GOP establishment circles, there were talks of
sanctions against California, of imposing economic consequences until it relented. There was talk of withdraw-
ing federal benefits from the state, including withholding
social security checks. The idea was to bring its economy
to its knees until it relented.

Online, a petition to send the 101st Airborne to Sacramento gathered 2 million signatures in thirty-six hours.
Within a week 8 million people had signed. The loudest
voices on the airwaves demanded immediate military
protection for California gun owners, immediate return of
all confiscated guns, and the payment of tens of millions
of dollars in reparations to citizens imprisoned under the

state's gun laws and the families of citizens killed in gun-law-related conflicts.

But there was one idea that united the moderate establishment and the more radical Republicans, a middle ground between merely hoping the crisis would pass and using the armed forces to crack down on dissent: arrest California's leaders.

Thus was born Operation Lincoln. The goal was simple. Following a contempt finding and issue of an arrest warrant for key California leaders, federal law enforcement would execute a coordinated multi-site raid to simultaneously arrest California's governor, lieutenant governor, and attorney general—each of whom was directly resisting the Supreme Court's ruling.

The arrests would be followed by the filing of yet another contempt motion against the new acting governor if that person failed to comply with the Supreme Court's ruling. The hope was that the sight of the leaders of the state in handcuffs would not just cow the next layer of California's leaders but also send a message to blue-state leaders in New England and on the Pacific Coast. The progressive populations of Oregon, Washington, Massachusetts, New York, Connecticut, and Rhode Island were all clamoring for their own states to pass versions of California's Save Our Lives Act.

But a nation divided means a bureaucracy divided, and shortly after the Department of Justice filed its contempt motion, planning details for Operation Lincoln landed on the front page of the *New York Times*, including helicopter insertion points, identities of the arresting officers, description of liberal rules of engagement that permitted arresting officers to open fire upon perception of a threat, and contingency plans for medical treatment of the governor outside of California in the event she was injured during the arrest. The *Times* even obtained copies of the briefing slides, running them alongside its own vivid animation, making the operation look not unlike the dramatic raid to kill Osama bin Laden.

Immediately, California protesters responded by forming human chains around the residences of every leading California politician. They vowed to rush any helicopter, any vehicle approaching that was not flying California's bear flag.

The president canceled Operation Lincoln. Instead, acting under the pretext of protecting California from the nonexistent militia threat, he launched an economic blockade—closing roads into the state and permitting only departures. He gave the governor ten days to reverse course, or else the president would impose an absolute economic shutdown on the state, including freezing state assets, stopping social security payments to California residents, and even refusing Medicare and Medicaid reimbursements.

Instead of these threats leading California to accede, the president once again faced litigation and injunctions. A San Francisco district court blocked the president's sanctions and ordered a lifting of the road blockade. The Ninth Circuit affirmed, and as the Department of Justice prepared its appeal, a coalition of progressive DOJ lawyers filed bar complaints against their conservative colleagues, claiming that the DOJ was arguing a frivolous case and acting in bad faith.

At every point, California's lawfare stymied the president. So his frustrated and furious congressional allies played their trump card. They killed the legislative filibuster and fast-tracked legislation granting the president sweeping powers to deal with the crisis, including the specific authority to declare a national emergency and impose extreme sanctions on any state declared—by executive order—to be in a state of insurrection. It also empowered the president to deploy the military and voided the Posse Comitatus Act, the law prohibiting the use of the military in law enforcement, in its entirety.

This was the point when the chickens of negative polarization came home to roost. A nation with a strong common culture could perhaps survive a crisis like this. More accurately, a nation with a strong common culture likely wouldn't reach such a crisis. A nation with a high degree of national affection and cohesion similarly could face the challenge. But what about a nation that increasingly lacked a common culture or mutual affection and was increasingly dominated by hate and fear?

It would crack. It did crack. And, like John Brown at Harpers Ferry, one radical family pushed Humpty Dumpty off the wall.

It happened on a rural road in Trinity County. Two California Highway Patrol cars were driving to a prearranged buyback point where a group of gun owners was taking advantage of a twenty-four-hour amnesty to turn in their weapons. Three miles from the destination, Brian Randolph and his sons Joseph, Martin, and Luke were waiting. They were armed to the teeth with AR-15s, semiautomatic shotguns, and pistols. They were wearing helmets and body armor. Perched on their helmets were GoPro cameras. As the police cars came into view, the Randolphs turned on their cameras and began live-streaming on every major social media platform in the United States.

Within three minutes of the first gunshots, more than 100,000 Americans were watching a brutal ambush. Within six minutes, the number jumped to a million. Before the last feed was shut off, more than 42 million Americans saw all or part of the bloody massacre of four police officers and the secondary ambush of the squad cars racing to their fallen comrades. By the time the firefight ended, six officers were dead and six were wounded. All four Randolphs survived, wounded, and were taken into custody.

The governor of California called a halt to gun confiscations to establish new security procedures. The non-gun-owning public panicked. To them, what had quickly come to be called the "Trinity Ambush" signaled the start of a guerrilla war. And they looked at the online reaction in red America with rage and fear. While there were certainly many millions of red Americans who were aghast at the brutality of the event (one of the GoPro shots featured a highway patrol officer begging for his life before he was executed in cold blood), many millions of others celebrated.

"This is why we need AR-15s."

"Rifles can stop the cops. The Randolphs just proved it."

"The president won't act, so Americans did."

"Six down, sixty thousand to go."

Sitting in her office in the governor's mansion, in a meeting with the lieutenant governor, attorney general, and California legislators, the governor turned to her colleagues and said the words that now echo in history.

"I don't want to belong to a nation filled with this much hate."

The next night, she delivered a televised address—perhaps the only address by a governor that was carried live nationwide on every broadcast, cable, and major online outlet. The contents of the speech had not been leaked, but one word had . . . *secession.*

"My fellow Californians," she began, "words cannot express the depth of my sorrow. Words cannot express the depth of my resolve. I mourn the lives lost in the Trinity Ambush. I mourn the lives lost in the towns and cities of this magnificent state. Children have lost their fathers. Husbands have lost their wives. And so long as this nation remains addicted to violence—addicted to its guns—men, women, and children will continue to die.

"But my mourning is not confined to our terrible casualties. I mourn the loss of the American idea. I mourn the loss of our democracy. And I mourn the fact that Washington is now occupied by men and women who live to hate, who would oppress you, and who would deny you the opportunity to build a society centered around the love, compassion, and justice that are central to the California values we hold dear.

"I used to believe that the arc of history pointed toward a redeemed America, a nation transformed, one that rejected its racist and violent past for a future of tolerance, inclusion, and peace. I know that the arc of history bends toward justice, but not everywhere—or at least not at the same time.

"Therefore, I have come to the conclusion that the time has come to form a new nation—one born not out of violence but through peace, a nation that is built from the ground up to respect the environment, treat its citizens with decency, and shun the war-making impulses that have cost the lives of countless millions. I am asking you to join me, but I am only asking. I am asking the president of the United States to permit us to leave, but I am only asking.

"There will be no Fort Sumter in California. There will be no armies of brothers and cousins facing each other in this beautiful land. This is my appeal to you—to think, consider, and then vote. Do you want to stay in the United States? If you do, then I shall yield. We shall repeal the Save Our Lives Act. We shall return guns to California's citizens, and we shall comply with all the orders of the illegitimate, undemocratic Supreme Court. We will submit to this president. Then I shall resign. My lieutenant governor will resign. So will the attorney general. You will elect a new governor, one committed to this nation, not the new nation of California that I hope we can build together.

"If you vote to leave, however, I shall present our petition directly to the president. I shall go to Congress, and I shall plead our case. I shall declare that our two nations will be friends, that we shall have an economic relationship, and that we will pledge to never, ever threaten their national security.

"And if they have any mercy in their hearts, if they have any remaining humanity or respect for our autonomy, then they will let us go. They will let us build the shining city on a hill that the United States used to believe it could be. We will beat our swords into plowshares. Freed of the obligation of sustaining the immense American war machine, we will return our resources to the people. We will repair our schools. We will repair our roads. We will invest in renewable energy. We will create the society that we've been prevented from building. And we will show the immense potential of the people of California.

"I know which path I want to take, but I leave the ultimate choice to you. The fate of our state, I place in your hands."

Across the United States, 2,731 miles away, the president of the United States watched the speech in the Oval Office. When it was over, he smiled. The governor of California had just saved his presidency. The governor of California had just guaranteed permanent conservative dominance of the United States. He hadn't said anything yet to any of his advisers, to the Speaker of the House, or to the Senate majority leader. But he knew.

He would let California go.

The president responded with four key political and strategic moves, each designed to facilitate the breakup of the Union on terms most favorable to red America.

First, he issued emergency orders removing every significant and immediately mobile American military asset from the Pacific coast, including every Pacific-based element of the American nuclear arsenal.

Second, he announced that in the event that California opted to remain in the United States, it would be placed under "temporary" federal control, for the purpose of ensuring "constitutional compliance."

Third, with the end of the legislative filibuster, he now had the ability to implement conservative legislation at will. So he proposed an ambitious legislative agenda that was specifically designed to be wildly popular with large majorities in the remaining states—including national legislation further protecting gun rights, ensuring national religious liberties, and mandating complete federal funding cutoffs for any medical facility that performs abortions.

Finally, if California voters decided to leave, he pledged to enter into a permanent defense relationship, guaranteeing the physical security of the new California Republic so long as it promised to remain largely demilitarized, with strict caps placed on the new nation's military forces— enough for the barest level of self-defense. In exchange for relieving California of its defense obligations, he would force California to implement an "open market" relationship with the United States. In other words, there would be no more tech company boycotts of individual states. California companies would be compelled to provide their products for American consumption, on pain of economic sanctions or withdrawal of the defense relationship.

Thus, when voters went to the polls, they had two choices—freedom or military occupation. They were voting for state prosperity or control by Washington. They were voting to preserve their way of life. They were voting to preserve the ability to govern themselves.

Ultimately, the vote wasn't close. More than two-thirds of Californians voted to leave, and within the year— facing the prospect of a permanent conservative supermajority government without California's congressional delegation or electoral votes—Oregon and Washington voted to leave as well. Congress consented, and a new nation was admitted to the United Nations, the American Pacific Republic.

California's action precipitated a decade of dramatic change. At the end of a ten-year span, five nations existed under one common economic union. The United

States flag had 34 stars, the American Pacific Republic had six regional governments, and the New England Alliance was comprised of ten former U.S. states. Together with Canada and Mexico, they formed the North American Economic Union. Only the United States, however, retained its nuclear deterrent. Only the United States remained a military superpower.

In the end, the American people did not suffer terribly from their disruption. Yes, as the three communities pulled apart there was economic dislocation and disruption. An estimated 20 million Americans moved from one new nation to another, solidifying the political culture of each place. It took years to sort through the financial and economic negotiations—including how to allocate the American national debt, how to shift the enormous financial obligations of the social safety net, and whether to maintain defense commitments abroad.

In the end, Americans proved to be perhaps just a bit happier after the breakup. Each nation had its own political struggles, and each nation had its own divisions. Utopia is not possible on this earth, after all. But there was, for a time, a burst of optimism, hope, and purpose. There was, for a time, a burst of energy as the people strove to build a nation stronger and better than their new rivals.

So one great experiment in freedom and democracy ended. Another great experiment began. Three cultures. Three nations. Loathing replaced by rivalry. Polarization replaced by purpose. As American power crumbled, the world rushed to rearm. Ancient enemies girded for new battles, but Americans? They mainly felt relief.

13

Texit

W hen he was sworn in as governor of Texas, Francisco Gonzalez had no idea he would become the first
president of a nation that critics derisively called the "New
Confederate States of America." He had fought secession.
He hated separation. But events forced his hand, and by
"events" he meant a movement started by the governor of
Alabama—a charismatic black Republican who believed
with all his heart that the defense of the unborn was the
greatest cause of his life.

Two years earlier, the Supreme Court had overturned
Roe v. Wade, and instantly the South and much of the
Midwest was transformed into an abortion-free zone.
The wave of heartbeat bills and trigger bills that had
previously passed in states such as Louisiana, Missis-
sippi, Alabama, and Georgia had spread throughout ev-
ery southern state except blue Virginia and purple North
Carolina. Texas had passed a trigger bill. Oklahoma and
Nebraska had passed heartbeat bills.

After *Roe* fell, protests had convulsed the big blue
cities of Texas, but in general the transition went
smoothly. There were few abortion clinics left in the
South or Midwest, abortion rates were very low and getting lower, and—truth be told—few citizens noticed a

meaningful cultural difference. The political difference, however, was profound.

Among the base voters of the South, there was an immense outpouring of cultural and regional pride. Labeled "deplorable" for so long, called "racist" for generations, they celebrated their place on the "right side of history." The historical equations were decisively reversed. In their telling, the region of slavery and Jim Crow was now the region of life and love. By contrast, the region of abolition and Union represented the culture of death and hate.

But there was no mistaking the fury and revulsion in blue America at the Supreme Court's decision—a fury compounded by the distinct regional division. To blue America, the South's distinctive stand had nothing to do with life and everything to do with its historical role as the most backward, most oppressive American region. There was no "culture of life." How could they claim that they respected life when they preserved the death penalty and had the highest infant mortality rates in the nation? How could they claim the mantle of social justice when they stood as a stubborn firewall against universal health care?

And so, as the presidential race approached, each Democratic candidate made a singular pledge—the assault on women's rights would not stand. Each Democratic candidate promised to expand the Supreme Court, to nominate new justices who would respect a woman's right to control her own body and restore *Roe*.

The Senate majority leader and every single blue-state Senate candidate signed a pledge to pack the Court, even if it meant ending the legislative filibuster. Purple-state Democratic Senate candidates balked, but when the economy entered a deep recession and a Democratic wave beckoned as the election approached, it became clear that for the first time in a generation, the Democratic Party was likely to control the presidency and both houses of Congress.

That meant no more filibuster. That meant single-payer health care. That meant Court-packing. That meant fundamental changes in constitutional law, including a dramatic revision of religious liberty doctrine. That meant that the nation's most religious region looked at a thoroughly secular party and determined that its way of life was under threat.

And it meant abortion was coming back.

The first black governor of Alabama was Jalen Jackson, a forty-year-old Southern Baptist adopted son of a desperate single mom. When his biological mother had learned she was pregnant, she had wanted to abort him, but she didn't have a car, and she couldn't find anyone willing to drive her two hours to the state's sole abortion clinic. While she tried to find her way to Birmingham, a Baptist volunteer at a crisis pregnancy center introduced her to a prosperous mixed-race Christian family in Montgomery. The husband was black, the wife was white, and they convinced her that they could love her son with their whole hearts and raise him with a strong black role model.

Jackson was a young teen when his adoptive parents told him his story, and he immediately became a passionate pro-life advocate. In fact, life was the defining issue of his political career. He first tried to join the Democratic Party, but the Democrats at the University of Alabama refused to tolerate his pro-life views. Infuriated by his activism, they required each and every member of the

College Democrats to sign a pledge to support "reproductive freedom" as a condition for belonging to the club.

He refused, they expelled him, and he walked straight into Republican arms. He joined the Republican Party at just the right time. It was increasingly open to progressive economic policies, but still steadfastly Christian and pro-life. His moderate economic policies and his African American identity meant that perhaps he could expand the Republican supermajority. His fierce dedication to life meant that he'd connect with Evangelicals. And his stand against Democrats meant that he was a "fighter."

He was elected to the statehouse right out of college. Then he ran for Congress. Four terms later, he was swept into the governor's mansion with a historic majority, and he immediately implemented what he called his "families-first" conservative agenda, an agenda designed to build what he characterized as a "culture of life," from conception to natural death.

In pulpits first across Alabama and then across the South, Jalen Jackson became the face of social change. He was keenly aware of his place in history, and his narrative became the South's narrative about itself. The South had turned the page. It was the guardian of life and liberty, and Alabama's governor was its ambassador to the nation.

But he had competition. In Texas, Governor Gonzalez was another new face of the New South, and his story was compelling also. He had been born into poverty as the son of an illegal immigrant (a fact used against him relentlessly by his critics). He served in the Marines, was deployed twice in the Marine infantry, and then attended the University of Texas on the GI Bill.

After graduation, he started a family, joined a small, struggling construction company as its in-house accountant, and rose to the position of chief operating officer in five years. Fifteen years later, he was its CEO, the company was worth hundreds of millions of dollars, and he was a pillar of the San Antonio community. Before he ran for governor as a Republican, his charitable efforts earned him the title of CNN "hero."

Governor Gonzalez represented a revamped Texas Republican Party. It was culturally conservative, yes, but it was also self-consciously inclusive. It was pragmatic. And it thrived in an increasingly diverse state, mainly because the blue urban Texas left had radicalized itself far beyond the zone of comfort for the mostly Christian suburban and rural right. Angry islands of blue lived uncomfortably within immense seas of red.

In Texas, the less-radical party won, and a pragmatic conservative like Gonzalez was always going to be less radical than the products of the Austin, Houston, or San Antonio Democratic machines.

The events that dissolved the United States are easy enough to describe and had been eminently predictable. Indeed, in hindsight they seemed inevitable.

First, an unpopular, recession-burdened president lost in a bigger-than-expected landslide. In spite of the Democrats' radical agenda, the Republicans lost most of the key swing states and lost the popular vote by a whopping 7 million votes. The blue wave extended into the Senate, where two upset victories over purple-state incumbents gave Democrats a fifty-five-seat majority, the largest majority in a generation. Democrats also retained control of the House, extending their majority to the largest gap since Barack Obama's first term.

Amid the euphoria of victory—and ringing press declarations of a "realignment" and expert assessments that the long-expected "emerging Democratic majority" had finally emerged—words of moderate caution were thrown to the winds.

On the first day of the new Congress, the Senate abolished the filibuster. By the time the new president took the oath of office, two long-planned and relatively simple bills were on her desk, ready for her signature. The first was the most comprehensive gun control bill in modern American history. The second expanded the Supreme Court to a grand total of fifteen justices.

That's when Governor Jackson stepped forward. At an emotional meeting of the Republican Governors Association, he extracted a pledge from every governor in the Deep South and multiple conservative midwestern states to use all of the available resources of state law to block enforcement of any federal law restoring abortion rights, removing religious liberty, or confiscating firearms.

The Lexington Declaration—so called because it was signed at the RGA meeting in Lexington, Kentucky—was greeted with volcanic fury by the left. The president called it lawless. Congress called it nullification.

Acting in response to employee demands, Silicon Valley reacted with one angry voice. It threatened to de-platform the websites of allegedly "intolerant" religious organizations and pro-life activists. Apple closed its stores in each state whose governor signed the Lexington Declaration for a solid week in protest. Disney yanked production from every state that had signed the declaration. Coastal banks pulled financing from multiple church construction projects. Some companies even went so far as to threaten to close manufacturing plants, and in at least two cases companies canceled industrial construction plans in the South.

Nothing stopped the cycle of escalation. Finally able to enact its long-blocked legislative agenda, the Democratic Congress didn't stop with gun control or packing the Supreme Court. It passed a version of single-payer health care. It passed an onerous carbon tax. It then crossed the red line, passing three bills that pushed the Christian conservative community into a state of panic.

The first, the Civil Rights Renewal Act, not only expanded and strengthened federal protections against discrimination on the basis of race, sex, religion, sexual orientation, and gender identity, it explicitly stated that any nonprofit entity violating the provisions of the act was not entitled to receive federal tax exemptions or any other federal benefit. Religious institutions that held to orthodox Christian or traditional Jewish sexual morality would lose their tax-exempt status.

Christian schools, charities, and churches faced a choice: change their policies or face potential financial catastrophe. Even worse than the financial blow, however, was the cultural signal—the federal government was declaring the Christian church to be the equivalent of the Klan.

Right on the heels of the Civil Rights Renewal Act, Congress passed the American Reproductive Justice Act, a statute that declared abortion regulation the exclusive province of the federal government and struck down every single state regulation or restriction on abortion. Abortion on demand—at any time from conception until birth—became the uniform law of the United States. The act even eliminated the Hyde Amendment and allowed for direct federal funding for abortion. The Democratic Congress wasn't going to wait on its new Supreme Court to reinstate *Roe*. It would do so under its own authority, secure in the knowledge that the new Court would uphold its extraordinary assertion of federal authority.

Finally, Congress took direct aim at the Lexington Declaration, passing the Insurrection Act, which imposed direct criminal liability on the governor of any state that attempted to enforce any act of (broadly defined) "nullification." The message to red-state chief executives was clear: assist the Democratic government in the execution of new laws or face federal prison.

Coming one after another—all passed on a party-line vote—these reforms hit red America like a shockwave. Congressional Republicans clamored for impeachment. Conservative media called it a coup. And Republican state legislatures responded with acts of direct defiance.

One by one, the core red states of the South and Midwest enacted the aims of the Lexington Declaration into law. Some went so far as to criminalize enforcement of what they deemed "unconstitutional" statutes within state boundaries. The states of Mississippi, Alabama, Louisiana, and Arkansas preemptively declared any ruling from the new, packed Court to be null and void.

In Texas, Governor Gonzalez watched and waited. The state was too divided, too purple to pass a version of the Lexington Declaration. His urban residents were in a state of rage against conservatives. His rural and exurban residents were livid at progressives, and the suburban swing voters anxiously wished for calm.

But calm was not to come.

Immediately the IRS sent a wave of letters to southern and midwestern religious nonprofits demanding to examine their policies protecting the rights of gay and transgender employees and students. Each entity was given ninety days to change its policies or face termination of its tax exemption.

At the same time, the president announced her six nominees to the Supreme Court. Immediately dubbed the "Social Justice Six," they represented the cream of the progressive legal crop. Each had a long record of progressive jurisprudence, and each had a glittering resume. Progressive Americans immediately called them the most qualified justices in American history. Conservative Americans called them the most radical. In protest of their nomination, Senate Republicans voted unanimously to boycott their hearings and boycott the confirmation vote.

The Senate GOP statement was simple and stern: "The Republican Party will not participate in the destruction of our Constitution. It will not lend any legitimacy to a nakedly authoritarian power grab."

The third thing that happened had nothing to do with religious liberty or with the Supreme Court. It was the colossal misjudgment, the colossal mistake, that tipped the balance in Texas and ultimately fractured the nation.

In late March, a mere four weeks after the president signed the Insurrection Act, the attorney general of the United

States—acting on his own authority—ordered the arrest of Governor Jackson. The proximate cause was a directive the governor had delivered the previous week to prevent the reopening of a long-shuttered abortion clinic in Birmingham. Alabama state troopers were posted outside the empty building, blocking Planned Parenthood contractors from entering and preparing the facilities for a reopening. This was a direct violation of the Insurrection Act. The law had to be enforced, or the law was meaningless.

Jackson was going to be outside Alabama, participating in a debate in Houston, in one of the bluest neighborhoods in one of the bluest cities in Texas. FBI sources indicated that he would be foolishly traveling with a light Alabama state trooper security detail, depending on Texas Rangers for most of his personal protection. But if an arrest was timed properly, the FBI could intervene at the governor's hotel, just after he arrived from his flight and just before the Rangers arrived to supplement security. The strategy was simple: move quickly, act decisively, and whisk Jackson back to D.C. to stand trial in federal court.

The plan went awry immediately. Through a cascading series of miscommunications, the FBI arrived too soon. Rather than seizing the governor as he checked in, a parade of federal SUVs pulled into the hotel driveway at high speed just as the governor's car arrived. One collided with his car, knocking it into the side of the hotel. In the confusion—and before the FBI agents could clearly identify themselves—the Alabama state trooper sitting directly beside the governor believed he was confronting an assassination attempt and opened fire at the first FBI agent to emerge from his SUV.

A hail of gunfire erupted from the federal agents, and by the time the smoke cleared, two Alabama troopers were slain, one FBI agent was seriously wounded, and—most critically—the governor of Alabama lay dead on the Houston pavement.

It was a moment of staggering incompetence. An ambitious attorney general had overreached, his operation had failed, and not even his resignation—not even a presidential apology—could prevent volcanic outrage in the American South, especially when conservative reporters noted that one of the FBI agents had tweeted "We got the bastard" just minutes after the governor was shot.

The next evening, the livid, grief-stricken governor of Texas went on television and declared his intentions. The state would join the Lexington Declaration. If the federal government intended to enforce its new laws, it would have to mess with Texas.

His words were crystal clear: "I am acting now to defend our constitution. I will protect the unalienable rights of Texas citizens, including the right to speak freely, worship freely, and protect their homes and families. I will not allow violent federal aggression in the borders of this state.

"Effective immediately, no Texas state or local official may enforce any order issued by the new, packed Supreme Court. Further, any federal official attempting to enforce any order issued by the new, packed Court will be subject to arrest. Any federal agency attempting to enforce any order issued by the new, packed Court will be subject to expulsion from sovereign Texas territory.

"I am taking this action by executive order, but I am asking the legislature to pass the Lexington Declaration.

I do this knowing full well that I place myself in violation of the Insurrection Act. I place myself at risk of suffering the same fate as my friend the governor of Alabama.

"But I swore an oath to preserve, protect, and defend the Constitution of the United States and the Constitution of Texas. I swore that oath. Those words bind me. That means that I have the individual responsibility and authority to preserve our fundamental constitutional liberties. I intend to exercise that authority.

"The next weeks and months will be trying times for this state. I recognize that we are defying federal authority, but that authority has been illegitimately and unconstitutionally exercised, in flagrant disregard for the liberties and the very lives of Americans on Texas soil. Our people are not pawns in a partisan Washington game, and I will not permit them to be treated as such. Texans' liberties are precious. Our lives are precious. And now they are under threat. Texas will stand against that threat, one state, united, so help us God."

The next week was pure political and legal chaos. The Texas legislature passed legislation based on the Lexington Declaration, and when it did, each and every previously wavering solid-red southern and midwestern state followed suit. All at once there was an immense regional bloc of defiance to federal authority, stretching from South Carolina on the East Coast to Utah in the Mountain West.

Faced with this level of defiance and provocation, the president acted. She issued an order nationalizing the Texas National Guard, placing it under direct federal authority and (she thought) preventing the Texas governor from calling it into service. At the same time, she asked the acting attorney general to prepare plans to arrest the governor of Texas, dissolve the Texas state legislature, and take direct federal control of the state.

Her reasoning was simple: seizing control of Texas was the key to quashing the emerging rebellion. There were millions of sympathetic progressives in Texas. There were millions of wavering suburbanites. Remove the toxic radicals, and perhaps calm could be restored, the momentum of the insurrection could be slowed, and the crisis could be resolved.

What happened next was entirely predictable to anyone who'd been following not just the worsening political crisis but also the long-standing and worsening cultural divides between red and blue. There was simply no way that a majority of Texas political leaders or a majority of the people of Texas would submit to a party or to politicians who they believed hated them and hated their way of life.

And so on April 21—coincidentally the anniversary of the decisive Battle of San Jacinto, the victory that had secured Texas's independence in 1836—the commander of the Texas National Guard refused the president's nationalization order and stated that he remained under the command of the governor of Texas. The next day the commanders of the state guards of Louisiana, Alabama, Arkansas, Oklahoma, and Mississippi followed suit, an act that placed them in a state of open, armed rebellion against the federal government.

Every single important political, cultural, and corporate figure then magnified the crisis. There were no "cooler" heads. There was no spirit of compromise. There was only hate and fury and fear. Declaring that a "red curtain" was descending on Texas, multiple Silicon Valley corporations announced a simultaneous boycott of the state. As if a switch was flipped, social media feeds across the state went dark. Websites crashed. Streaming video services stopped. The few websites that remained live were soon flooded with traffic and messages, mainly howling with fury at progressive censorship.

The president—long distrustful of a military establishment whose members, she knew, largely voted against her—panicked. She immediately demanded pledges of loyalty from senior military officials and impulsively demanded the removal of officers from Texas from positions of command—an order that was reversed hours later (when she was frantically reminded that some of America's most vital military bases were in Texas, often staffed and commanded by men and women who'd grown up in Texas or in military families that spent much of their lives in Texas).

Short-lived as it was, the order caused immense anger in the ranks. And that anger triggered even greater paranoia in the White House. White House officials looked at a map of military bases and saw that they were disproportionately spread across the exact states that were rebelling: Fort Hood and Dyess Air Force Base in Texas, Barksdale Air Force Base in Louisiana, Fort Benning in southern Georgia, Fort Campbell in Kentucky. Even the nation's ICBM force was spread out in deep-red states. The president's advisers feared an avalanche of military disloyalty.

In blue America, no one was calling for calm. In blue America, they demanded law and order. They compared the national moment to the days before the rebels fired on Fort Sumter. Leading public figures thundered about "neo-Confederates," and congressional leaders demanded the wholesale arrest of governors, national guard officers, and anyone else engaged in insurrection against the United States. In Texas, blue-city protests in Austin, Houston, and Dallas turned to riots, and as city police cracked down, angry voices called for the "liberation" of Texas's minority population from "white power."

The absence of normal social media communications channels and the flickering websites meant that traditional news was replaced with wild rumors, and Governor Gonzalez struggled to maintain communication not just with his constituents but also with the rest of his government. Reports of violence in the cities were exaggerated and distorted, and false stories of multiple shootings and other acts of violence spread across the South and Midwest. Citizens turned their televisions to local broadcast channels, and the state government commandeered local networks in the effort to maintain public order.

Desperate calls to Silicon Valley leaders went unanswered. Progressive tech billionaires channeled their even more progressive "woke" workforces and thundered their condemnation, adopting the exact language of "neo-Confederates" that had spread across the progressive world.

Faced with a communications blackout, spreading unrest in the cities, and growing anger and fear in the suburbs and rural Texas, Governor Gonzalez acted once again. It was his turn to escalate. He invoked emergency powers to seize the physical assets of every boycotting corporation, allocated state resources to bring the internet back online, and authorized economic reprisals against "hostile" corporate entities. The Texas legislature and multiple additional state legislatures rushed to pass laws criminalizing "economic terrorism" by coastal corporations and authorizing the arrest of any employee who didn't comply with state orders to lift boycotts or resume normal economic activity.

Texas authorities seized server farms, raided offices, and commandeered even retail outlets. Any and all financial assets in Texas possessed by companies boycotting Texas were immediately seized.

In solidarity, citizens across red America launched their own boycotts. All at once, Silicon Valley moguls lost a full quarter of their domestic customer base. But they could not even consider compromise; their uniformly and resolutely leftist employees would not permit it. This was suddenly the social justice struggle of their lifetimes, and they were no more willing to see the sweat of their brow benefit "bigots" than the soldiers of the Texas National Guard were willing to see their own efforts harm their friends and neighbors.

In fact, the Silicon Valley action remained so immediately consequential to Texans that it eclipsed federal action in importance almost immediately. Mothers had trouble contacting their children. Companies couldn't fill orders. Hospitals had difficulty accessing online medical records. The corporate boycotts felt like an actual attack on the state, and the outpouring of fury was directed at all progressives, not just the specific offending corporations.

The straw that broke the camel's back, however, happened in Louisiana, not Texas. Even as the president was paralyzed by the crisis—unsure how to respond when the tools of law enforcement or military control seemed to be slipping out of her hands—Pentagon officials issued their own orders. Though they hoped the crisis would pass, out of an abundance of caution they quietly directed that the military secure all nuclear assets in the "zones of instability." That meant Texas, yes, but it also meant each state where the national guard remained under state control. And that meant flying strategic bombers (and their inventory of nuclear-tipped missiles) out of Barksdale Air Force Base in Louisiana.

The commander of the 2nd Bomb Wing, Colonel Brian Brenner, a farm boy from Mississippi, disobeyed the order. Invoking the wing's motto, "Libertatem Defendimus" (we defend liberty), he and a half dozen other aircrews diverted to Texas, carrying with them multiple nuclear-tipped missiles, and placed them under the command of the governor of Texas.

Brenner's action had ripped off the festering scab of military partisanship in the most dramatic way possible. The negative polarization of the larger nation had slowly but surely wormed its way into the heart of the armed forces. In 2018, a former senior adviser to President George W. Bush observed that "the general rule of thumb with the military is that it moves along with public opinion but lags conservative."

This truth meant that the military was a more conservative mirror of the rest of society, and its conservatism was supplemented by an increasing degree of regionalism. The disproportionate concentration of bases in the South had given the military a distinctly southern sensibility, as even men and women from California and New York spent entire careers (and raised families) shuttling from Texas to Kentucky to Georgia and back again. New York dads raised southern kids, and those southern kids then had a higher propensity to enlist when they became adults.

And so once Colonel Brenner made his move, the dam broke. Virtually the entire 3rd Cavalry Regiment in Fort Hood signed a statement of intent not to take up arms against the state of Texas. The senior leadership of the 1st Cavalry Division made a similar pledge. Across the length and breadth of southern bases, similar pledges popped up in platoons, companies, battalions, and brigades. They would confront the enemies of the United States abroad. They would not, however, serve to oppress their fellow citizens. And since the pledges were sprinkled throughout the entire military force, there was no single active-duty unit that the president could unequivocally count on to impose order in Texas, or anywhere else.

In hindsight, the Columbus Conference—a meeting between the president and the Texas governor that was conducted in an atmosphere of intense suspicion and extraordinary security, with the Secret Service blanketing the president and a large, heavily armed contingent of Texas Rangers surrounding the governor—was doomed to fail. Even if either leader wanted to compromise, their constituents would not permit it. At the start of the crisis, only the fringe conservative cranks were demanding division and Texas independence. Within six months, however, secession was the Texas consensus, and it was a growing consensus in deep-red America.

At the start of the crisis, only the fringe progressive

cranks were demanding that the Democratic president arrest the Republican governor and declare martial law. Within six months, that was the progressive consensus. And the progressive consensus was that compromise with Texas was compromise with neo-Confederates. Social justice was at stake. History was watching.

But there was something else at work—something that historians later rightly focused on as critical to the failure of the talks. A growing movement of conservative Christians began to believe—empowered by viral videos that rocketed through the makeshift southern social networks—that the time had come for southern redemption. No, this was not the Old South rising again to oppress, but a New South rising to liberate and to end America's second great sin. It was time to ban abortion. It was time to stop the slaughter of innocents.

And God, in his divine providence, was allowing the very region most guilty of America's original sin not only to repent of that sin but also to become the abolitionists of a new nation. Leave the killing (and God's judgment) to the progressive American remnant. Justice (and God's favor) would rest with the new, independent republic, a republic of life.

This sentiment was viewed as truly deranged—even medieval—on the American left. Not only were progressive writers, politicians, and celebrities secular, they often didn't even know any people of faith. To them, conservative Christianity was superstitious at best and malicious at worst, a "religious" pretext for underlying hatred and bigotry.

But in regions where men and women still disproportionately attended church—and with church attendance spiking in a time of deep anxiety and uncertainty—the vision of a free nation truly dedicated to liberty and to life fired the imagination. Just as revivals swept through the Confederate and Union armies during the Civil War, a revival furor swept through the rural and exurban South, eventually capturing the imagination even of worshippers in the suburban megachurches.

Crisis brought two American communities not to the middle but to the extremes. Generations of loathing turned into white-hot rage. And so, while the president and governor shook hands when they departed neutral ground, there were no smiles. There was no joint statement. There wasn't even a press conference. The president took off first, on Air Force One, with a fighter escort. The governor followed in his own plane, informally dubbed "Lone Star One," surrounded by a phalanx of F-22 Raptors that had defected from Langley Air Force Base.

When Gonzalez landed, he was solemnly greeted by a delegation from the Texas legislature. In their hands they carried a resolution of secession. With the governor's signature, he'd initiate a secession process—to begin in the legislature and then to be put to a statewide vote.

The resolution carried the legislature, then passed the popular vote by 58 to 42 percent amid widespread voter boycotts in Houston, Dallas, and Austin.

The new Republic of Texas was launched on January 1. In the next months the Lone Star flag gained additional stars as neighboring states decided there was no place for them in a United States that—without Texas—would be dominated by progressive governments. By June 15, the first wave of secessions was complete, and at each stage civil war was averted by a simple reality: the cost of war was too terrible for either side to contemplate.

The lethality (and rapid deployability) of modern weaponry averted civil war, but the brinksmanship that ensured the new nation's existence left the two nations angrily divided, in a state of cold war, subject to economic boycotts and travel bans. This was no amicable split, but rather a bitter divorce.

A great migration commenced. Millions of Americans left their homes, uprooted their families, and moved to more hospitable ideological and religious territory. The United States became more secular and more progressive. The Republic of Texas (later the American Constitutional Republic) became more religious and more conservative.

Negative polarization had reached its endgame. One superpower had become two.

14

A World on Fire

The moment the United States split apart, every world leader knew a single, simple truth: Pax Americana was over. The peace that had been maintained through the overwhelming military and economic might of the United States would not hold. The security guarantees of a confused and broken nation meant nothing. Carrier battle groups that previously had ruled the seas sat in port while the new, opposing nations of the North American continent negotiated their fate.

American squadrons returned home as their pilots and crews chose sides in the Great Divorce. The portion of the North American continent that retained the name "United States of America"—while still economically powerful—was simply incapable of maintaining the military force or the security guarantees of a united nation, especially in the year following the split.

The United States tried to maintain deterrence in hot spots like South Korea, but rival great powers knew that the United States was in no condition to project meaningful force overseas. Even worse, the entire Western alliance had grown utterly dependent on U.S. logistical assets to move any kind of significant force beyond their own borders. Britain's two carrier battle groups and France's single aircraft carrier were insufficient to maintain any deterrent posture in the Far East, and they were barely adequate to project any real strength in the Atlantic.

Thus arrived a period that Russian and Chinese military planners quickly dubbed the "golden years." They knew that the divided American nations would eventually settle on a security strategy. They knew that allied powers would ramp up their own military spending and eventually replace a large portion of the lost American power. But the key word was "eventually." This would take time.

Modern weapons—including aircraft, main battle tanks, and ships—are extraordinarily complex. They can't be produced at scale immediately, even if panicked national governments authorize emergency procurement programs. The divided American nations arranged hasty sales of pre-positioned equipment, but it would still take time to recruit and train men and women to operate new weapons.

Consequently, China believed it could reclaim Taiwan without triggering a conflict with the United States. Russia knew that it could swallow the Baltic states and the Russian ethnic enclaves in southeastern Ukraine while NATO remained paralyzed. Russia moved first. Latvia and Lithuania fell to an influx of "little green men"— Russian soldiers in unmarked uniforms and vehicles— who took key airports and city centers within seventy-two hours, with hardly a shot fired.

Estonia was different. Estonia resisted fiercely, and so it received the full weight of the 8th Guards Mechanized Corps. The conflict was intense but brief. In one week, the Russians secured every major population center. In three weeks, every element of the Estonian military larger than a company was destroyed. After a month, only small bands of partisan fighters remained, and they could mount only sporadic attacks.

NATO did nothing. It could do nothing, aside from engage in furious denunciations and impose (ultimately short-lived) economic sanctions. The UN was utterly ineffectual, with China joining Russia to veto any meaningful Security Council resolutions. American airpower had largely returned home. American naval assets were in port in North America. And without American support, neither Britain, France, nor Germany could project any meaningful force to Estonia or any other Baltic state. So they stayed put rather than face sure, bloody defeat.

A Russian-engineered coup toppled the Western-allied government of Ukraine, and just like that, NATO withered. The old Eastern Bloc nations realized their vulnerability and—over time—entered into new security and trade agreements with their old Russian "allies." Russia regained control of its near abroad, the old great power rivalries flared again, and for the first time in nearly a century, the world noticed the stirrings of German militarism as Germany rearmed as fast as possible to face a renewed and immediate Russian threat.

Events in Europe were destabilizing, but with the exception of thousands of dead in Estonia, they were relatively bloodless. The cost was largely strategic and economic, as the disruptions of the Great Divorce gutted Western economies even as they faced substantial new defense obligations.

The Far East wasn't so fortunate. From the moment Chinese planners saw the United States reneging on its

NATO commitments, they knew that Americans would not and could not aid Taiwan. There was not a single American carrier at sea west of Pearl Harbor. Not a single American surface ship was in position even to offer itself up as a "tripwire" to trigger an American response.

And so China determined to transform its "one China" policy from political fiction to practical fact. It demanded Taiwan's surrender as it began an immense, open, and obvious military buildup across the Taiwan Strait. The intent was clear—to convince Taiwan that resistance was futile.

But Taiwan had advantages that Estonia did not. First, there was the significant matter of the roughly hundred-mile-wide strait separating the island from the mainland. The second was the fact that Japan was shocked out of its isolation at the prospect of a united, hostile China with no American ally present to guarantee its security.

Japan mobilized its undersized (though technologically advanced) military, warned China against aggression, and then reached a fateful decision—to race to develop a nuclear deterrent. In spite of its unique history as the target of the world's only atomic attacks, Japan knew that it had to rely on its own power to guarantee its security, and when facing a nuclear-armed China, Japan needed its own deterrent, urgently.

China believed that Japan was bluffing. Its planners refused to believe that the nation would transition from ingrained pacifism to outright militarism so quickly, and in the absence of any direct threat to Japanese sovereignty. So China pressed ahead.

Taiwan rejected China's demand for surrender as decisively as possible. Working with the Japanese military it re-created the surprise attacks of 1941 at scale, with the most modern and sophisticated weapons money could buy. China's open preparations, designed to cow its rivals into submission, turned into the nation's military Achilles' heel. Japanese military doctrine, from Port Arthur to Pearl Harbor, emphasized the importance of the first strike, and strike first it did.

In part because of Chinese mistakes (after all, it had not fought a major conflict against a first-rate power since the Sino-Soviet border clashes in 1969) and in part because of Japanese tactical brilliance, Japanese and Taiwanese pilots achieved almost complete surprise. Missile and air strikes arrived virtually simultaneously, sinking Chinese naval craft and blanketing Chinese air bases with explosions. In a single day, Japanese and Taiwanese forces rendered an amphibious assault virtually impossible.

Humiliated and furious, Chinese leaders refused the immediate offer of peace and launched a massive conventional air and naval counterattack designed to destroy the Japanese and Taiwanese militaries, crush their economies, and make them sue for peace. Thus began the most significant Pacific air and naval conflict since World War II, one that eventually also drew Australia into the fray—while a wary South Korea mobilized its reserves and remained neutral as two old foes fought bitter battles in the seas and skies all around.

For months air raid warnings were routine in many of China's and Japan's great cities. Commercial shipping ground to a halt. International trade crashed. Chinese forces fully invaded and occupied Hong Kong. The global economic disruption that had been called the "American Recession" after the Great Divorce became the "Pacific Depression" as two of the world's largest economies ground each other into the dust in the midst of an all-out air and naval war.

After maintaining a public posture of ambiguity regarding its nuclear program—an ambiguity designed to deter Chinese escalation—Japan dramatically announced its entry into the nuclear club with an underground test of a substantial 250-kiloton device. South Korea quickly followed suit. Taiwan indicated that it reserved the right to build its own bomb. Australia did not test a weapon, but it formally withdrew from both the Nuclear Non-Proliferation Treaty and the Comprehensive Nuclear Test Ban Treaty—two documents that had become all but meaningless in world affairs. The world began a round of runaway nuclear proliferation, as advanced nations in multiple world regions reached for their own arsenal of ultimate weapons.

In the meantime, the conventional war raged on. Slowly but surely, the Japanese gained superiority in the sky and on the seas. The Taiwanese air force, lacking either the F-35 or the F-15, struggled to defend its home island, but the Japanese exacted a fearful toll on Chinese aircraft, shooting them down far faster than Chinese industry could replace the losses. One by one, the Japanese sank China's few aircraft carriers, and after six months of conflict, the Chinese navy was crippled, with its surface ships rarely venturing out from their heavily guarded ports.

A land war in China was unthinkable. Neither Taiwan nor Japan wanted to commit an entire generation of young men to large-scale ground combat, so the goal was air and naval superiority, followed by economic strangulation.

The war reached its end stage just as Japanese and Australian forces launched an ambitious series of amphibious landings designed to seize each and every disputed island in the Spratly and Senkaku island chains. With Chinese aircraft chased from the skies and the Chinese navy largely at the bottom of the sea, a military and economic noose was tightened in the South China Sea and East China Sea. Large sections of China were routinely plunged into blackout conditions by relentless attacks on the nation's power grid, and economic deprivation was creating internal unrest.

Desperate to stop the fighting, China rattled the nuclear saber. It declared that the continued invasion of Chinese-claimed territory and the continued air strikes on the Chinese mainland represented an existential threat to the nation's existence. Firebrands inside China urged leadership to use its nuclear arsenal while it still possessed a strategic edge—claiming that while China could absorb terrible losses, Japan would be effectively destroyed by a Chinese attack.

Unwilling to repeat the traumas of 1945, Japan stood down. It agreed first to a cease-fire in place, then to a negotiated withdrawal from seized Chinese territory— based on a Chinese agreement to completely demilitarize its disputed island possessions. China refused to enter into a lasting peace agreement with Taiwan. There was only an armistice. A humiliated China raced to rebuild its decimated navy and air force. In response, Japan built up its own air and naval forces to a size and power not seen since its days of empire.

As for Taiwan, it effectively declared its independence from China by successfully testing its own hydrogen bomb and building its own nuclear arsenal.

Europe and Asia were not the only flash points. With America in full retreat, Iran attempted to sprint to its own nuclear bomb, a move blocked—at least temporarily—by a series of Israeli air strikes that triggered Hezbollah rocket barrages into northern Israel.

With the eyes of the world focused elsewhere, Israel responded with overwhelming military force, unleashing its full arsenal on Hezbollah positions, invading southern Lebanon yet again, crushing Hezbollah, and driving its remnants out of missile range of Israeli civilians.

For the first time since Israel's war for independence, there was no international outcry. The great powers were panicked by the reality and danger of much larger conflicts much closer to home. Saudi Arabia was quietly pleased at the blow to Iranian power, and after Hezbollah's initial missile volleys, the militant group proved ineffectual in the face of a fully mobilized IDF.

By the time the reduced United States and the new nations of North America reconstituted truly functioning militaries, reached sustainable security agreements, and began to claw back from economic depression, the world had changed. It was as if the clock had spun back more than a century, to the multi-power world that existed before the First World War—except with more great powers, more potential flash points, and far more terrible weaponry.

In 1914, the great powers had been concentrated in Europe, with Japan rising in the East. Now India, China, South Korea, Taiwan, and Japan all possessed formidable economies, growing militaries, and nuclear weaponry. China still coveted union with Taiwan (and revenge for its humiliating defeat). South Korea increasingly considered forceful unification with the unstable North. Japan and China nursed their ancient grudge, and Chinese and Indian forces clashed along their disputed boundary.

Back home in the old United States, global instability damaged economic prosperity. Americans who had once decried globalism and scorned American alliances now saw and experienced the high cost of lost international institutions. But even the terrible war in the Pacific seemed distant. A nation in the midst of dissolution had no time for worry about far-off conflicts. It pulled back into itself, dealt with its own upheaval from the great internal migrations, and each new North American division generated its foreign policy only after it fought back to economic stability.

Truth be told, there were Americans who liked the new world. They had always resented international dependence on American arms and American lives. They were glad to pull back to their new borders and had little interest in crises overseas. They saw the new nations as more in keeping with the intentions of the original Founders of the old United States, avoiding foreign entanglements and staying out of foreign wars. Freed from the burden of defending the world, the new nations believed they could pour their resources into their own people. Standing armies diminished. The new navies still sailed the seas, but the fleets were smaller. There were fewer carrier battle groups. There was no need to project overwhelming force, only to deter attacks.

And so the world settled into its new reality. Great-power conflict was no longer unthinkable, shifting alliances played havoc with international travel and international trade, and world economies became more unstable. Militaries abroad planned for future conflicts that Americans hoped and believed would not reach across the oceans to touch their shores. Isolationist and polarized Americans had broken the world their forefathers made, and they could not, ever, put it back together again.

III

To Save America, Chart James Madison's Course

15

Pluralism, a Beginner's Guide

The scenarios outlined in the preceding three chapters represent a projection of what may happen if the polarizing trends I've outlined in this book continue unabated while the nation is subject to foreseeable, even predictable severe stress. The Calexit scenario is based on existing progressive fears that minority rule (empowered by the Senate and the Electoral College) will degrade national legitimacy at the same time that continued right-wing extremism degrades progressive self-governance.

The Texit scenario, by contrast, is based on existing conservative fears that majority rule—unmoored from the principles of the founding—will discard the Bill of Rights, fundamentally rewrite the Constitution, and destroy conservative liberty and conservative communities.

At the heart of both scenarios is the fear that your political opponents don't just hate you, they want to *rule* you. They want to dominate you. This was the right-wing intention announced in the influential *First Things* essay I discussed in the beginning of the book—to "fight the culture war with the aim of defeating the enemy and enjoying the spoils in the form of a public square re-ordered to the common good and ultimately the Highest Good."

This is the left-wing intention (and prediction) expressed

in "The Great Lesson of California in America's New Civil War."[1] This essay, by Peter Leyden and Ruy Teixeira, was one entry in a lengthy four-part series called "California Is the Future," and it bleakly posited that there is "no bipartisan path forward for America." Leyden and Teixeira wrote that America is divided between two competing economic systems, classes, and cultures, and that one has to win while the other has to lose.

In their words, "America today has many parallels to America in the 1850s or America in the 1930s," and they argue that "both of those decades ended with one side definitively winning, forming a political supermajority that restructured systems going forward to solve our problems once and for all." The Republican Party won the Civil War "and then dominated American politics for 50 years." Conversely, in the 1930s, "the Democratic Party won and dominated American politics for roughly the same amount of time."[2]

The perspectives in those two essays represent the fundamental view that the way through the American divide is to fight and win. The central idea of this book, by contrast, is that, thanks to increasing geographic separation and group polarization, the "fight and win" approach to the American divide won't produce a permanent settlement but rather will result in more extremism and more division—extremism and division that can lead to dangerous instability.

The "fight and win" approach is consistently seductive, however. Why? In part because, due to the regularity of American elections, one side can always feel like it's winning. Democratic euphoria after 2008 gave way to Republican exultation after the Tea Party landslide of

2010. The cycle of agony and ecstasy is extraordinary. Republicans had an apocalyptic view after 2012, then were full of hope after 2014, in abject despair before Trump's surprise win in 2016, and then rattled again after 2018.

Yet while the partisan mood moves up and down, the underlying American divide grows wider, and the stakes of each election feel higher. The result is that each election result carries with it the risk of not just irrational exuberance ("We've discovered the key to victory!") but also irrational fear ("We're doomed!").

Lost in the quest for total victory—and the corresponding profound fear of defeat—is the understanding that our nation is doing *exactly the wrong thing* to confront the "violence of faction" that James Madison warned about in Federalist No. 10 (and which I discussed in detail in Chapter 1). Increasingly, our nation is attempting to control fractiousness by removing its causes from only one side or the other, rather than by controlling its effects.

In some cases, competing factions are attempting to destroy the liberty that is essential to the existence of our nation's divisions, and in their quest for total victory they seem intent on "giving to every citizen the same opinions, the same passions, and the same interests." This is the quintessential fool's errand. This is the cure that's worse than the disease.

But this cure is so alluring in part because it *seems* right. After all, if your opponents aren't merely misguided but rather actively evil, their destruction is unquestionably a net public good. Your quest to win the culture war and drive your opponents from the public square is a fundamentally virtuous cause. Moreover, that quest can provide you with a powerful sense of meaning and purpose.

This kind of polarization, when combined with the "big sort," actively bonds a community.

But remember that Madison charted a different path. He reminded us that liberty is essential to political life and that the quest for uniformity is futile. "As long as the reason of man continues fallible," Madison says, "and he is at liberty to exercise it, different opinions will be formed."

That is especially true when the body politic consists of people from so many different faith backgrounds, from so many different national cultural traditions, and—frankly—from so many different geographies. Where someone lives—an urban, suburban, exurban, or rural area—often materially shapes that person's attitudes and outlooks. In such a circumstance, the quest for uniformity is futile, and the restrictions of liberty that are so tempting to those who seek uniformity are far more inflammatory and divisive than they are edifying or unifying.

So let's get back to the answer we previewed in the first chapter—Madison's embrace of pluralism, whereby "the increased variety of parties comprised within the Union, increase [its] security." By protecting the liberty of our citizens, including by protecting their rights to form free and voluntary associations, we are not only increasing the ability of diverse human beings to find community and purpose within the body politic, we are limiting the ability of the state or any private faction to gain the overwhelming power necessary to reasonably believe that it can achieve dominance.

To be clear, embracing pluralism requires that people surrender very little. You can still seek to shape your local community to reflect your political values. You can still seek to persuade the wider community to abandon beliefs and views—even religious beliefs and views—that you believe are wrong and destructive. You can even continue to seek the national ascendance of your political faction. To embrace pluralism, citizens truly need only to embrace two real limitations on their quest for ultimate ideological victory.

First, if you are a citizen of a pluralistic, liberal republic, you need to defend the rights of others that you would like to exercise yourself—even when others seek to use those rights to advance ideas you may dislike or even find repugnant. The right of free speech has independent value, for example. So does religious liberty. Due process has immense value even if deployed in defense of a guilty man.

These rights represent civic and moral goods worth defending, and they are the rights that provide each individual with hope for fairness and change regardless of the outcome of any political contest. They are the rights that stand as a firewall against political violence exactly because they provide that hope for change. No citizen should feel that their only recourse to achieving the justice they deserve or the liberty that is their unalienable right is by picking up the rifle in their closet.

Second, if you are a citizen of a pluralistic, liberal government, you should defend the rights of communities and associations to govern themselves according to their values and their beliefs—so long as they don't violate the fundamental rights of their dissenting members. American liberty and the American Revolution were never about radical individual autonomy. They were never about smashing institutions for the sake of liberating the individual.

In other words, the American Revolution was no French Revolution. It was no cultural wrecking ball that sought to sweep away entirely not just the old form of government, but also the national faith itself, replacing it with the cult of reason. Instead, in many ways, it was an effort at cultural preservation, with the colonists' rights grounded in their understanding of the rights of English citizens and their rage rooted in the denial of those rights.

The American Revolution—with its core principles codified in the U.S. Constitution—combined individual liberty with deep respect for the network of sovereign states and communities that constituted the new American nation. The original Constitution left intact a system of federalism, for example, that would be virtually unrecognizable to an American today. It did more than just preserve churches, it affirmatively protected them from state domination or subjugation.

These ideas aren't just powerful, they're proven. When you wed liberal democracy to intact families, strong civic engagement, and virtues of self-discipline and self-restraint, you can unleash prosperity and innovation unlike anything the world has seen before. Moreover, not only can those virtues persist through centuries of liberalism, they're amply rewarded by the liberal structures themselves. While it's fashionable to despise America's immense, meritocratic upper middle class, that class also happens to contain the population that is more likely to cling to marriage, to family, to church, and to education.

But liberalism and pluralism falter in the face of hatred and intolerance. If you affirmatively hate another person, it is extraordinarily difficult to muster up the energy to lift a finger to defend that person's rights. It's instead easier to attack those rights with great zeal. If you despise another group, you have zero desire to preserve or protect their communities. Instead, you'll find the mere effort to persuade them to change their ways to be weak and inadequate. The temptation to use the coercive power of the state to marginalize them and push them to the edges of society will prove too strong to resist.

This is politics as "war and enmity." This is the mindset that sets a nation on a course that leads to the nightmare I saw in Iraq—where militants from two competing sides, carrying the weight of years of deep and abiding grievances, engage in a deadly battle for primacy. But when the two competing sides are motivated by their deepest beliefs and values, there is no outcome that results in true primacy. You can't even kill or torture a people out of their deepest beliefs.

We are not Iraq, of course. We have much tighter civic bonds. But our civic bonds frayed before, and they're fraying now. We're still human beings. We're not fundamentally better than the men who faced one another at Missionary Ridge on the last day of the Battle of Gettysburg. We have not evolved out of our capacity for hate and division.

I'm a realist, and that means that a book about division is not going to conclude with a call for love. And while a revolution of affection for our fellow humans would represent an extraordinary development in the life of our nation, I'm not nearly naive enough to believe one is imminent, and I'm certainly not foolish enough to believe that any single political figure—or even any collection of cultural and political leaders—can bring about such a revolution.

Instead, let's start modestly. Let's start with the absolutely most basic building block of reconstructing a commitment to liberalism and pluralism. Let's start with a term that conservatives have grown to hate and all too many progressives abuse and misunderstand. Let's start with tolerance, properly understood.

16

Rediscover Tolerance

I f you're a conservative, as soon as you read the word "tolerance" you were likely already alienated. "Tolerance" is the progressives' word. It's how they describe their own ideology, an ideology that can be remarkably intolerant toward conservatives—especially people of conservative faith.

If you're a progressive, you might look at the chapter heading and reasonably believe that I just urged everyone to be like you. After all, isn't the progressive movement the home of tolerance and inclusivity?

No, it's not. And neither is the right. We've forgotten what tolerance actually means, and tolerance—properly understood—could at least begin to offer a cure for the disease of negative polarization.[1]

So what is the true version of tolerance? Not long ago a psychiatrist who writes under the pseudonym "Scott Alexander" produced an illuminating piece describing the distortion of tolerance in modern American discourse.[2] He cleverly outlines how tolerance has simply come to mean "I like historically marginalized groups" and nothing more. In other words, he describes how a person on the left might advertise their tolerance by broadcasting their regard for "gays, lesbians, bisexuals, asexuals, blacks, Hispanics, Asians, transgender people, and Jews."

But Alexander next posits one question to liberals that cuts to the heart of the matter and demonstrates why they don't truly understand what tolerance means: "Well, what do you think is *wrong* with gay people?"

Their answer would be immediate: "What do you think I am, some kind of homophobic bigot? Of course I have nothing against gay people."

If that's the case, then progressives are not *tolerating* anything. The word "tolerance," of course, implies that there is *something to tolerate*. True tolerance, according to Alexander, is "respect and kindness toward members of an outgroup"—not respect and kindness toward members of what others would define as an outgroup, but rather respect and kindness toward people who are out of *your* group. When there's nothing to forgive, nothing to overlook, and no patience required, there's no tolerance.

Most people mistake tolerance for fellowship, agreement, or tribalism. The result of this flawed understanding is that millions of people believe—to the very marrow of their being—that they're something they're really not. They have taken the vice of their particular brand of tribalism and transformed it into the false virtue of fake tolerance.

Though they'd be shocked to learn that one of the defining characteristics of their lives is a fiction, others can see it quite clearly—especially victims of their so-called tolerant ways. In fact, widespread liberal intolerance in the name of tolerance is the stuff of parody on the right. The satirical site *Babylon Bee* recently announced Coexist, a (fake) new product line for "anti-fascist" progressives, over an image of a Molotov cocktail branded with a Coexist sticker. The article went on to announce other new (fictitious) riot tools, like Coexist rocks, baseball bats, and ski masks.

Yes, of course that's extreme, and most liberals are aghast at the violence of groups like antifa. But many are not. And there are even mainstream media voices who've compared the masked mob to, yes, the American GIs who stormed Omaha Beach on June 6, 1944.[3]

Yet academia and the elite media place an enormous amount of emphasis on this fake version of tolerance. They proudly proclaim that they reserve the right to be intolerant to preserve the tolerant ethos of the community. In one of my favorite First Amendment cases, I sued a university that declared in no uncertain terms, "Acts of intolerance will not be tolerated."[4] Yes, it used those exact words. And those words were and are typical of college campus speech codes. Sadly, the "real world" is becoming more like the college campus, where dissent is often seen as inherently hateful, the dominant group ideology is presumed to be virtuous, and there is increasing intolerance toward the idea of even working next to people you believe hold differing views—no matter if they have never mistreated any colleague at work or elsewhere.

Entire corporations are now adopting the ideologies and norms of the most ruthless campus social justice activists, ruining careers and depriving employees of their livelihoods when those employees dissent from the dominant ideology. Doubt me? Let's look at one of the most powerful corporations in the world, and let's do it through a story that resonated throughout the political right but barely made a ripple in the wider progressive world—the story of a Google employee named James Damore.

(Incidentally, I often find it the case that while people on the left and right may generally know about the same events—sometimes even by one name, a name like "Damore" or "Covington Catholic" or "Kaepernick"—they have much different understandings of the facts, and of the importance of that event to their friends and fellow citizens on the other side of the aisle.)

Like many corporations in Silicon Valley, Google has a diversity problem. Its workforce is disproportionately male. It has trouble recruiting female software engineers, for example, and despite long years of effort in crucial categories, women are woefully underrepresented in key areas.

In response to this challenge, Damore wrote an internal memo that challenged his company's diversity policies and offered an alternative method of achieving diversity—one that he claimed would reach coveted diversity goals without discriminating against men to elevate women who wouldn't otherwise be competitive for the job.

Citing recent research about the differences between men and women, his lengthy memorandum pushed back on the idea that disproportionate male representation in tech fields was the result of invidious, malicious discrimination. Instead, he suggested, the disparity was the result of individual choice and innate distinctions between men and women. As he told *Wired*, the memo caused considerable internal debate. "Before it went viral, responses from coworkers ranged from 'I totally agree' to 'Is this true?' or 'I disagree because . . .'"[5] When his memo was made public, people argued more passionately over his conclusions. Some agreed with Damore, others vigorously disagreed. Some were livid.

Now, in a workplace that's actually tolerant—under the proper meaning of the term—the memo would have generated discussion and debate and nothing more than that. After all, unless there is evidence that Damore had discriminated against or mistreated women at the workplace, his memo represented a good-faith effort to solve a corporate problem. And given Google's long-standing commitment to tolerance, diversity, and inclusiveness, you might imagine that his treatise would've been received well (or at least thoughtfully) by Google executives. They should love an open discussion about important matters that concern their employees.

Indeed, they should have been open to Damore's ideas in part because a number of social scientists backed up Damore's conclusions. He wasn't just spewing uninformed biases. He was engaging with actual research. For example, the consulting company Accenture and a group called Girls Who Code released a fascinating study pointing out that fully 82 percent of computer science majors were male.[6] In fact, the share of women choosing computer science majors had *decreased* since the early 1980s in spite of significant increases in the share of women in college overall and startling gains in economic opportunity in the tech field more broadly. Moreover, there was no evidence of systematic discrimination in college computer science departments that would have led to such a stark, nationwide trend.

According to the study, women were quite simply choosing to do something else, and their sharp turn away from coding could be traced all the way back to the end of junior high. The report found that girls' interest in tech peaked in middle school; by high school, not only did girls typically not enjoy the field, but their friends felt the same. Not all girls, certainly, but many, and they didn't start to recover their interest until college.

If disparities in given fields are the result of free choice, are the disparities inherently problematic? If people are free to choose, will men and women make the same choices in the same proportions? And aren't these questions valid enough to be worth at least a conversation?

But no. The *intolerant* social justice left (not the entire left, of course) has charted its course. It has reached definitive conclusions about the purpose of its movement, and it's not to reach proportionate gender or racial equity across all professions. It's not everyone succeeding in the same ratios in every field. If that were the case, then you would see gender studies professors lamenting the decline in white male academic achievement compared to women. You'd see social justice activists protesting about fields where white males are underrepresented.

Instead, the principle that ultimately emerges is this: When cultural or gender distinctiveness works favorably for a marginalized group, that's a cause for celebration. When cultural or gender distinctiveness yields unfavorable results, the very existence of meaningful difference is denied and oppression is to blame.

No one denies that actual gender discrimination still exists. No reasonable person denies that the legacy and reality of American racism are responsible for many of the disparate outcomes that plague important American professions. But as we work steadily and relentlessly to cleanse our culture of racism and sexism, are we certain that every American identity group will make the same choices, in the same proportions, as every other group?

Rather than engage with Damore, however, Google summarily terminated him—without presenting any evidence of workplace misconduct beyond the fact that he shared his ideas.

After Damore was terminated, he fired back against Google with an extraordinary legal broadside, a 181-page complaint arguing that Google's corporate culture encourages, sanctions, and facilitates an immense amount of abuse against conservative white males.[7] He included screenshots of internal Google communications and postings on internal Google message boards that would have constituted strong evidence of hostile-environment race and gender harassment if the races and genders were reversed.

For example, "Googlers" (that's what employees call themselves, using Google's corporate language) relentlessly enforce a "Googley" culture in which employees blacklist conservatives (by blocking them from in-house communications), actually boo white male hires, and openly discuss committing acts of violence against political opponents.

In one posting, an employee proposed a "moratorium on hiring white cis heterosexual abled men who aren't abuse survivors." In another, an employee advertised a workshop on "healing from toxic whiteness." Another post mocked "white fragility." The examples go on and on, for page after page. Damore also alleged (and again, provided screenshots of emails and other communications to support his claims) that managers actively attacked conservative employees, encouraged punitive actions against dissenters, and even awarded "peer bonuses" for speech attacking conservatives.

At the same time, Googlers exhibited a remarkable level of tolerance for certain types of unusual behavior. For example, Damore claims that "an employee who sexually identifies as a 'yellow-scale wingless dragonkin' and an 'expansive ornate building' presented a talk titled 'living as a plural being' at an internal company event." (To be clear, Google should be welcoming for dragonkin *and* conservatives—so long as the dragonkin and conservative do their jobs well and treat colleagues with dignity and respect.)

The screenshots and images presented a compelling prima facie case of racial and gender bias that would have been intolerable and illegal in the vast majority of American jurisdictions, including under federal law. American civil rights law is generally color-blind. In other words, it protects white employees every bit as much as it protects black employees, and conduct that would be unlawful if applied to African Americans or women is also unlawful if applied to whites or males.

Google is, of course, disproportionately male. But in the company's efforts to diversify its workplace, it may not commit unlawful acts of discrimination or make explicitly discriminatory hiring and firing decisions in any given department. In addition, California (unlike many states) provides a limited degree of protection against political discrimination. Damore cited California labor codes that prohibit employers from "controlling or directing, or tending to control or direct the political activities or affiliations of employees," and from coercing or attempting to coerce "employees through or by means of

threat of discharge or loss of employment to adopt or follow or refrain from adopting or following any particular
course or line of political action or political activity."

The evidence Damore provided was damning, and
not just because it raised legal concerns about Google's
behavior. The cultural implications are profound. For a
generation the American public has been conditioned to
think of Silicon Valley as a special place where American
ingenuity is at its apex. Silicon Valley billionaires have
enjoyed special status, and the men and women who work
creating the apps and devices that have changed our nation are often seen as America's best and brightest, the
lovable nerds who enrich all our lives.

Now we see a different side to the story: Googlers may
have special coding skills, but much of their discourse
represents a special kind of pettiness and intolerance toward many of the Americans who eventually buy or use
their technology. They are often fact-free, insulting, and
narrow-minded. In other words, a Silicon Valley monoculture produces exactly the kind of discourse produced
by monocultures everywhere.

Yet, sadly, this culture isn't unique to Google. Talk
to Americans in industries ranging from software to
insurance and beyond, and you'll hear tales of internal
naming, shaming, and even social media monitoring that
privileges one side of the debate and considers conservative discourse inherently problematic.

I have conservative friends even in Nashville who ago-
nize over their social media posts while their progressive
colleagues hold forth without fear. In progressive corporations, conservatives are often held to the highest standards of civility and reason, while angry, threatening

progressives are merely deemed to be full of "righteous indignation."

This kind of culture doesn't exist everywhere. There are countless thousands of workplaces free of such bias. But to those who claim that campus social justice warriors will be humbled when they encounter the "real world," I give you Google. Sometimes social justice warriors change the real world, and when they make it "Googley," they often make it more intolerant and ignorant than the campuses they left behind.

The United States is a better country not only when the government protects the right of free speech, but also when the *culture* values that right. Yes, even companies should value the free exchange of ideas as a default. Free speech is the essential liberty—the liberty that helps preserve all others—because without the ability to call out unconstitutional actions you cannot possibly maintain a free nation. In other words, Americans must be tolerant of dissent, even when they believe dissenters are offensive and wrong.

Talk to conservatives, and they'll often eagerly agree: it's the *left* that's intolerant. They know stories like Damore's. They're familiar with Jack Phillips, owner of Masterpiece Cakeshop in Denver, Colorado, who was charged in 2012 with discriminating against a gay couple when he refused to custom-design a cake for their same-sex wedding.

His case went all the way to the Supreme Court. The Court ruled 7–2 in favor of Phillips, finding that people should not be bullied or banished from the marketplace because of their religious beliefs about marriage.[8] A victory for liberty and tolerance, right? Yes. But not a total victory, not when the culture is so toxic, not when activists actively seek to punish opposing views and make the lives of their opponents as miserable as possible.

In June 2017, Colorado lawyer Autumn Scardina called Masterpiece Cakeshop to request a custom cake that was blue on the outside and pink on the inside.[9] The occasion, Scardina told the bakery's employees, was to celebrate her birthday, as well as the seventh anniversary of the day she had come out as transgender. Masterpiece Cakeshop ultimately refused Scardina's order on religious grounds. Two weeks after Jack Phillips won his first case at the Supreme Court, the Colorado Civil Rights Commission ruled that there was probable cause that Phillips had discriminated against Scardina on the basis of gender identity.

These cases—along with countless other cases on college campuses and in corporations from coast to coast—have taught conservatives a clear lesson. They have advanced the narrative that declares that progressives want to dominate, to destroy the conservative way of life. Progressives want them to shut up. And if conservatives don't shut up, progressives want them demoted, fired, or economically ruined. And since progressives control the heights of American culture, they have disproportionate power to impose their will. They're different from the right. They're *worse* than the right.

So when conservatives gain the heights of power, they'll be more tolerant, right?

Not exactly. Just ask a few hundred members of the National Football League.

Can Anyone Pass the Tolerance Test?

January 1942 was quite possibly the lowest point for American arms in the history of the United States. Much of the striking power of the Pacific fleet had been sunk or disabled. The Bataan campaign was under way, and it would ultimately result in arguably America's worst military defeat. Nazi Germany dominated Europe, Japan was on the offensive across Southeast Asia, and civilization itself hung in the balance.

You think we live in troubling times now? *Those* were troubling times.

It's against that backdrop that the West Virginia Board of Education passed a resolution requiring that a salute to the flag become a "regular part of the program of activities in the public schools." It made sense. The nation was rallying for war. We were in the grip of a total mobilization unlike any conflict in the nation's history. At the height of the war, a staggering 37.5 percent of the nation's gross national product would be dedicated to defense. A much smaller population than America has today would ultimately put 16 million men under arms. Patriotism was essential. If America didn't unite, it might die.[1]

A small group of Jehovah's Witnesses, however, declined to salute. Though they were patriots, their conscience wouldn't allow them to demonstrate the required reverence for the flag. They risked punishment and persecution for their stance, and appealed to the federal courts for aid. In 1943, with the outcome of the Second World War still very much in doubt, the Supreme Court rendered its verdict—with words that have echoed through the generations:[2]

> If there is any fixed star in our constitutional constellation, it is that no official, high or petty, can prescribe what shall be orthodox in politics, nationalism, religion, or other matters of opinion, or force citizens to confess by word or act their faith therein.

> Those are the most famous words of *West Virginia State Board of Education v. Barnette*, one of the Supreme Court's greatest cases, and these words apply today as well.

> Nevertheless, we apply the limitations of the Constitution with no fear that freedom to be intellectually and spiritually diverse or even contrary will disintegrate the social organization. To believe that patriotism will not flourish if patriotic ceremonies are voluntary and spontaneous, instead of a compulsory routine, is to make an unflattering estimate of the appeal of our institutions to free minds.

In other words, the power of the salute lies with the choice to salute, and the most repugnant form of censorship is compelled speech—the effort to force a person to state what they do not believe. Mandatory reverence isn't reverence at all.

The Supreme Court's words have a profound *cultural* meaning that resonates far beyond the letter of the law. The government cannot force an individual to violate their conscience. Nor should it try to bully powerful private entities into doing what the state cannot legally accomplish. Private corporations should think twice before using their own economic and cultural power to enforce conformity, even if they are legally empowered to censor their employees. Again, the cure for bad speech is better speech, and free speech cannot flourish in the midst of a culture of censorship.

When I share those words in conservative circles, audiences applaud enthusiastically. They see censorship as the province of the left, and they profess to long for greater freedom and greater room for dissenting speech.

But what happens if conservatives are confronted with speech that offends them? What if that speech is in a form that's especially triggering to conservative patriots? If leftist football players kneel during the national anthem, will tolerance reign?

In September 2017—to thunderous Republican applause—the president of the United States repeatedly called for the punishment of American citizens for exercising the very right guaranteed by *Barnette*: the right to refuse to salute the flag. Or, more precisely, the right to modify their salute to the flag. He told the cheering crowds: "Wouldn't you love to see one of these NFL owners, when somebody disrespects our flag, to say, 'Get that son of a bitch off the field right now. Out. He's fired. He's fired!'"[3]

And he did not stop.

In an October 17, 2017, interview with Fox News host Sean Hannity, President Trump said, "You cannot disrespect our country, our flag, our anthem. You cannot do that."[4]

Oddly enough, many members of the right endorsed Trump's language and message. "Fight fire with fire," conservatives said.

You mean censor in the name of freedom?

"Give them a taste of their own medicine," they yelled.

You mean act like a hypocrite?

And if you challenge the hypocrisy, you're often told that the double standard is a test of strength. "You just don't have the guts to fight the culture war," you're told. "You're a peacetime conservative"—once again echoing the language of war and enmity that marks much modern political rhetoric.

Yet when you try to silence people who don't have the same opinions as you do, you're contributing to a culture of finger-wagging shame instead of a robust, confident America. If football players—or any American—stand for the flag and the anthem, they should do so because of their love for this nation, its people, and its ideals, not because they fear the consequences of dissent.

In the words of the Supreme Court, do not make an "unflattering estimate of the appeal of our institutions to free minds." Seek to impose your will, and more people will kneel (if they're permitted); if they rise, it will be with resentment in their hearts. Embrace liberty, and not only will more people rise, they'll do so with joy. I wanted those players to stand. I wanted to see their hands over their hearts. But I wanted to see that happen out of love, not fear. And so long as the fear remains, a decision to stand means nothing but an empty victory in a culture war that will tear this nation apart.

In conversations with angry conservative friends, I responded with a thought experiment: How would you have reacted if Democratic president Barack Obama had called on the NFL to fire praying football player Tim Tebow because he was "injecting religion into football"? The answer was obvious to most of them: it would be more evidence of the left's intolerance, more evidence of the left's anti-religious bigotry—even though many of the same arguments apply. After all, Tebow publicly prayed on company time. He inspired some customers, yes, but he offended others. NFL owners have the "right" to prohibit public religiosity at private events.

Conservatives are solidly behind Masterpiece Cakeshop in its battle against forced speech. They are also outraged when private corporations and private universities enforce rules on speech that systematically disadvantage and silence conservatives.

But then a GOP president acts in the same manner, and their response is fist-pumping approval. Where is the tolerance? Couldn't just the slightest forbearance ameliorate negative polarization?

Raise this point, however, and the response is swift: "We'll stand down when they stand down." Yet since we're dealing with cultural forces and not competing armies, there is no "we" and "they" who can reach agreement. Sean Hannity and Rachel Maddow could host a peace summit in the halls of the United Nations, and talk radio would shriek at Hannity's betrayal and progressive Twitter would cancel Maddow. A cultural problem created by competing mass movements requires a mass movement in response. It requires individuals who are willing to go first, to model tolerance and rally Americans who long for tolerance. It requires injecting dissenting voices into the "group deliberation" I outlined in the first section of this book—dissenting voices who may agree on the ends of American policy but disagree that those ends justify intolerant means.

So, is there hope for an actual movement focused around mutual forbearance? Given all the trends I've been outlining at book length, the honest answer is "probably not." But it isn't "certainly not." There is at least a little bit of hunger for American grace and American tolerance.

Can Moments of Grace Make a Movement of Grace?

G iven the spirit of our times, things could have gone so differently. On November 3, 2018, *Saturday Night Live* cast member Pete Davidson mocked Texas Republican congressional candidate Dan Crenshaw's eye patch, saying he looked like a "hit man in a porno movie."[1]

Making fun of politicians is a *Saturday Night Live* tradition; even their looks are fair game. But this incident was a little bit different. Crenshaw, a former Navy SEAL, has his eye patch because he was terribly wounded in Afghanistan. Oh, and Davidson knew it, too. At the end of the bit, he said dismissively, "I know he lost his eye in war or whatever."

It wasn't funny. The joke was lame. It was also a partisan political gift to Crenshaw. A liberal comic had gone too far. He mocked a man who was maimed in a horrific IED attack, an attack that had taken the life of his interpreter and nearly blinded him for life. He mocked a courageous man's pain. And thus Crenshaw had attained the rarest position for a Republican politician: the status of aggrieved victim. He was free to swing away.

Instead, he refused to be offended. He noted that

the joke was bad, but his handling of the whole affair was—as the *Washington Post* described—"cool as a cucumber." Then *Saturday Night Live* called. The show wanted to apologize, and they wanted Crenshaw on the air. He said yes.

What happened next was the act of grace heard around the nation. Davidson came on the "Weekend Update" set and offered his apology, and then Crenshaw joined the set.[2] He took some good-natured shots at Davidson—Crenshaw's phone had an Ariana Grande ringtone (the singer had recently and very publicly broken off her engagement with Davidson), and he mocked Davidson's appearance—but then things took a more serious turn.

Crenshaw briefly spoke of the meaning of the words "never forget" to a veteran, saying that "when you say 'never forget' to a veteran, you are implying that, as an American, you are in it with them." Then he addressed his next words to Davidson: "And never forget those we lost on 9/11—heroes like Pete's father. So I'll just say, Pete, never forget."

Davidson's father was a firefighter. He died trying to save others when Davidson was a young boy. In one moment, Crenshaw not only honored a true hero but also softened American hearts toward Davidson, casting him in a new light. He's a man who carries his own pain.

It was a biblical moment. Crenshaw paid tribute to a man who could have been a political enemy. He was kind to a man who had been cruel. And no one could call this Navy SEAL's actions "weak." He had proved his courage. In fact, he showed a different kind of courage. He directly defied the prevailing partisan pressures.

It turns out that there's a market for grace in American politics. Within minutes, clips of the apology and Crenshaw's tribute to Davidson's dad rocketed across Twitter. Within forty-eight hours, a YouTube clip of the moment had accumulated more than 5 million views.

In a long *Washington Post* profile, Crenshaw spoke of the distinct trail he wants to blaze in a polarized age. Speaking of President Trump, he said, "His style is not my style. I'll just say that. It's never how I would conduct myself. But what readers of the *Washington Post* need to understand is that conservatives can hold multiple ideas in their head at the same time. We can be like, 'Wow, he shouldn't have tweeted that,' and still support him. . . . You can disapprove of what the president says every day, or that day, and still support his broader agenda."[3]

In other words, being a politician is not the same thing as being a partisan. It is not the same thing as being tribal. It is indeed a sign of our times that grace is so rare that a single moment can capture the attention of our nation, but the fact that it did capture that attention grants a degree of hope.

But only a degree. In 2019 I had the opportunity to speak with Congressman Crenshaw, and he indicated that he was already disillusioned. The sheer partisan bitterness had taken him aback, and while he was still committed to showing grace, he wasn't convinced that grace and courtesy had any effect. Even worse, in 2020, Davidson publicly expressed regret for apologizing to Crenshaw. A marvelous moment happened. Then it was lost.

But moments of grace do keep happening, and when they happen, their very virality demonstrates that a market for kindness does exist. But the moment happens, and then it's gone. Lost in an ocean of political bitterness and rage.

I've focused on Dan Crenshaw, a conservative who showed grace. But do we remember when Ellen DeGeneres defended her friendship with George W. Bush? DeGeneres and her wife, the actress Portia de Rossi, were filmed sharing a stadium suite (and affectionate laughs) with the former president at a Dallas Cowboys game.

DeGeneres is progressive. Bush is conservative. DeGeneres is gay and married. Bush opposed same-sex marriage. In "normal" life, friendships between conservatives and progressives aren't uncommon. In public life, such friendships are taken as a sign of moral compromise. So DeGeneres faced a wave of withering criticism. How *dare* she befriend an ideological enemy—especially one so powerful, one so destructive?

So Ellen had her own viral moment of tolerance.[4] On her show she addressed the controversy head-on. "Here's the thing," she said. "I'm friends with George Bush. In fact, I'm friends with a lot of people who don't share the same beliefs that I have." She continued, "When I say, 'Be kind to one another,' I don't only mean the people that think the same way that you do. I mean be kind to everyone."

Her explanation rocketed across the internet. On Twitter, her plea for kindness racked up 21 million views. And then, just as quickly as it came, it went, hastened out the door by angry partisans. Writing in the *Washington Post*, Molly Roberts declared that "Ellen DeGeneres [told] America she's better than us." In her piece she echoed right-wing culture warriors by denigrating kindness as a secondary virtue—or perhaps not even a virtue at all. "DeGeneres cries 'kindness' to explain herself because kindness is her brand," Roberts argued. "It's also an awfully clever brand to have. It has the heft of virtue without any of the heaviness that comes with actually being virtuous."[5]

The virtue, according to this position, is in the underlying policy position. The virtue is in being right. Kindness to powerful wrong people thus normalizes their perfidy. It grants them a degree of comfort they do not deserve. In this moral formulation, Christ's commands to love your enemies and to bless those who persecute represent dangerous wrongthink that can only lead to more oppression.

While there are many millions of Americans who appreciate and respect Crenshaw's and DeGeneres's acts of tolerance, they do not control the levers of cultural and political power. Their voices are lost in Washington, lost in Hollywood, lost online, and lost in America's political class. The political class exploits grace. The political class treats it as weakness. Thus, while parts of the public may long for mutual respect and a deescalation of partisan vitriol, even weary partisans don't want to show weakness. The people who actually drive American politics and policy are committed to escalation, and as they escalate, they drive their committed followers into ever-greater frenzies.

Even worse, these partisans are driven by mistaken views of their political opponents. They believe those opponents are far more radical than they truly are. Partisans tend to believe that large majorities of their political opponents have extremist views, when in reality extremists are still a minority in both competing political parties.

In fact, a study from the More in Common project found that "most partisan, politically active Americans . . . have deeply distorted perceptions of the other side." Indeed, the groups with the widest "perception gaps" were the "Progressive Activists and the Devoted Conservatives— the most ideological and committed groups of Democrats and Republicans."[6]

Remarkably, the more media people consumed, the more wrong they were about their political opponents. They weren't better-informed; they were misinformed. By contrast, those individuals who consumed the least media were the most accurate. Why? Perhaps because they were more likely to obtain their understanding of the other side's opposing views through actual friendships and human relationships rather than through cherry-picked news stories that often highlight only the worst expression of the other side's point of view.

In 2006 liberal blogger Kevin Drum asked his readers to come up with a term for what he called the "moronic practice of trawling through open comment threads in order to find a few wackjobs who can be held up as evidence that liberals are nuts." An anonymous responder came up with the term "nutpicking," and it's a perfect expression of the dominant discourse online.[7] It's virtually the business model of Twitter.

The process now works like this: In the midst of any significant world event or any interesting turn of the news cycle, angry partisans will open their Twitter apps and immediately start scanning the feeds of opposing politicians, celebrities, and pundits to look for an outrageous comment, preferably a comment celebrating death or violence. Inevitably, they'll find something ridiculous, in part because there are always some people who are angry enough to be ridiculous or because there are some people who essentially role-play their rage and absurdity for clicks and fame. Then, once the tweet or post is found, it rockets around the conservative (or progressive) online world as proof that "they" want you dead, or "they" want to strip away all your rights, or "they" barely think you're human. This process would be comical if not for the fact that it's constantly engaged in by the very people who are often the most influential, most powerful, and most politically engaged Americans.

But there is a silver lining to this dark cloud. America doesn't need very much tolerance to survive and thrive. While we can hope and wish for fellowship, America wasn't built to need fellowship, or even affection, to maintain its national unity and its immense national strength. It requires *just enough* tolerance and affection to permit other individuals to enjoy their most basic liberties and— critically—to permit other communities to (mostly) govern themselves. You don't even have to give up the dream of persuading all your opponents to abandon their ideas and philosophies. You merely have to give up the idea of coercing your opponents into holding (or at least living according to) "the same opinions, the same passions, and the same interests" that you deem just.

You have to embrace the idea that your fellow citizens— even those who disagree with you—should feel at home in this land. George Washington was particularly fond of a biblical passage from the book of Micah. He used it almost fifty times in his writings. The passage even made it into the wildly popular musical *Hamilton*. The words represent a clarion-call challenge for a nation that sometimes feels as if it's coming apart—"Everyone will sit under their own vine and under their own fig tree, and no one will make them afraid."

How can we make this hope a reality? The Founding Fathers can show us the way.

To Go Forward, We Must Go Back

There is no five-point plan for restoring the most minimal and basic forms of American tolerance. There is, however, a model for what that minimal tolerance looks like, codified into law. If the Bill of Rights represents tolerance of individual difference and a diverse civil society, federalism represents tolerance through self-governance and community autonomy.

These realities are so obvious that perhaps one of the single most frustrating things about our mutual hatred, our furious anger, and our extreme fear of the other side is that the solution is available, it's easily described, and it's right there in the Constitution of the United States. It's the eighteenth-century solution to our twenty-first-century problem. It would deescalate national politics, reinvigorate self-governance, and restore a world where every vote undoubtedly counted. Every citizen would have a meaningful voice in the life of their community.

Yet nobody really seems to believe in federalism. Each side is hypocritical about it, and the will to power continues to trump any temptation to let, for example, California be California and Tennessee be Tennessee. The best version of the nationalizing impulse is embodied by the idea that California progressives believe their policies are best for conservative Tennesseans, or that conservative Tennesseans know how to make progressive California freer. The worst version of this impulse is far baser, rooted in the simple desire to rule.

But neither misplaced idealism nor the desire for dominance fully explains the parties' reluctance to embrace true federalism. As is the case with most deep-seated cultural and political trends, there are some very good explanations for why that reluctance exists. And so it is with centralization and the long-standing bipartisan rejection of true federalism. American centralization is a response both to a terrible failure of federalism and to the dramatic external, existential threats of the Axis powers and the Soviet Union.

Let's focus first on the failures of federalism. In the popular American imagination, phrases like "state sovereignty" and "states' rights" conjure up memories of slavery and Jim Crow. It was the fierce independence of the southern states in defense of white supremacy and their "peculiar institution" that challenged the very existence of the American union. It was the later fierce dedication to white supremacy by those same states that maintained Jim Crow for a terrible century after the end of the Civil War.

It's the paradox of the American founding that but for the promises of federalism, our constitutional republic would not exist. Yet it was federalism that was also the bulwark of our nation's original sin of slavery and its continued sin of de jure racial segregation and discrimination. In the case of America's history of race discrimination, federalism enabled evil. Many Americans have not forgotten.

Moreover, also within recent American memory is the overriding necessity of unprecedented national mobilization to confront first Nazi Germany and Imperial Japan and then to maintain deterrence against the Soviet Union. These actions bound Americans together in a shared national identity, for a time bonded us to our national government—typically through its most capable instrument, the armed forces (which tossed tens of millions of Americans into a melting pot of shared experience and purpose)—and necessitated the creation of immense national structures and institutions to retain the military might to confront our geopolitical foes.

In fact, the sense of national emergency dates back to before these military challenges—to the Great Depression and to the decision to hand the reins of government to a man, Franklin D. Roosevelt, who intended to mobilize the government to combat an economic crisis. Consider that in a period of just under thirty years—from the launch of Social Security on August 14, 1935, to the creation of the modern military-industrial complex in response to World War II and to wage the Cold War, and to the beginning of Medicare and Medicaid on July 30, 1965—our nation created the vast centralized government that clings to us today. In less than thirty years, our federal government fundamentally displaced the reality that had held for most of the previous 160 years, rendering itself more important to a person's life than the state and local governments that used to matter the most.

The consequences have been profound. During a brief burst of time—and in response to highly unusual historical events, combined with a unique period of confidence in the national government—our nation created immense, permanent bureaucratic, administrative structures that together account for approximately 75 percent of our nation's $4.4 trillion budget and almost equal the whole of our nation's state and local government budgets.

Yet since the creation of those structures, our national situation has changed rather dramatically. No longer does one entire region of the country systematically suppress its black citizens. No longer do we face an existential threat to our very existence from a hostile foreign power that matches (or arguably exceeds) our military capability. No longer do we have the same degree of confidence in our national institutions that they enjoyed in the afterglow of victory in global conflict and postwar economic dominance.

Even worse, we now have decades of experience with the enormous bloat of government, and with the fear and anger that follow the transfer of such extraordinary power in a polarized society. Moreover, this takes place against the backdrop of a new way of living for Americans, one in which (as discussed previously) they are increasingly accustomed to considerable customization in their personal lives, from entertainment choices to precise matching with like-minded mates and the geographic "big sort" that creates like-minded enclaves.

And yet, even as we crave localism and customization in our consumer and residential lives, all too many of us stubbornly resist the idea that the federal government should follow suit, that it should grant greater autonomy to state and local governments—so that progressives like Nancy Pelosi are less relevant to Tennesseans and conservatives like Ted Cruz are less relevant to Californians.

Yet the failures of the past still haunt the present. I want to return to the same conference I mentioned earlier—where a group of us gathered to discuss and address American polarization. At one of the sessions, the conversation focused mainly on how to foster greater political moderation in the public, an exercise I thought (given the trends I've discussed at length in the opening chapters of the book) to be utterly futile. So I asked a question: What about rediscovering federalism? What about conforming our government to our cultural trends and rediscovering local control?

A thoughtful progressive friend immediately responded. "It's hard," he said, "to give up on the notion that embracing federalism doesn't also mean abandoning African Americans in Mississippi or to consigning the poor in red states to a harsher and more desperate life."

My response was immediate: "What kind of place do you think modern Mississippi is?"

I didn't respond that way to argue that Mississippi or Tennessee or Texas was in any way a perfect political paradise. There are pockets of real poverty in the Delta, and the Appalachian region is still—as my former colleague Kevin Williamson calls it—the "Big White Ghetto." Instead, I merely wanted to point out that there is both a quantum difference between states (then and now) *and* a huge gap between blue-state perception and red-state reality. A healthy federalism—one based on the development of constitutional law in the past half century—would be fundamentally different from the perverted federalism of the Jim Crow past.

Healthy federalism would correct the fundamental

error of the past. Prior to the passage of the Civil War amendments and their enforcement through Supreme Court precedent, the protections contained in the Bill of Rights were unavailable to marginalized Americans in oppressive states and regions. They didn't enjoy the right to free speech or to free association, and they were systematically denied rights to due process. They were shut out of the most basic American social compact—the guarantee of individual liberty.

Under healthy federalism, American citizens would enjoy guaranteed civil liberties that didn't waver or vary from state to state *and* they would enjoy a much greater degree of local control. The fundamental social compact would remain intact for all citizens, but public policy would be variable, customized for local interests and local values.

What's not to like? What's the downside?

The downside, of course, is that the rebirth of federalism necessitates the death of very particular dreams—the dream of dominance and the dream of utopia. The downside, of course, is that the rebirth of federalism involves standing by and *consenting* to your ideological opponents in different jurisdictions enacting policies and practices you may despise and consider unwise or unjust. It requires us to consent to political defeats inflicted on our ideological allies who are minorities in different jurisdictions. There are conservatives in California who would live in a more progressive state if we embraced federalism—just as there are progressives in Texas who would live in a more conservative state if we allowed for greater local control. And when we hate our political opponents, the idea that they could enjoy any triumph—even one far from our homes—is often intolerable.

Let's consider, for example, immigration, an issue that exposes incredible federalist hypocrisy on both the left and the right.

Immigration Breaks
the Federalist Will

In 2017 the California legislature passed three bills that together essentially declared that the state would dramatically limit its participation in the enforcement of federal immigration laws. The first bill, Assembly Bill 103, empowered the state to review and inspect state, local, and private locked facilities used to house noncitizens "for purposes of civil immigration proceedings in California."[1] Federal authorities use a number of non-federal facilities in the course of immigration enforcement in California, and now those facilities were subjected to heightened state scrutiny.

The second bill, known as the California Values Act, prohibits state and local law enforcement officials (with some exceptions) from voluntarily providing information about the release dates of individuals in state or local custody unless the individual has been convicted of certain, defined crimes.[2]

Finally, the third bill, the Immigrant Worker Protection Act, prohibits private employers from permitting immigration enforcement officials to enter "nonpublic places of labor" without a judicial warrant and prohibits them from voluntarily allowing enforcement officials to "access, review, or obtain the employer's employee records" without a subpoena or judicial warrant.[3]

When read together, the bills provide formidable sanctuary-state-style protections for illegal immigrants in California, but they *do not* prevent federal agents from doing their job. They prevent state officials (and private citizens) from actively cooperating with those federal agents. A federalist would say that these acts represent classic expressions of state values. A federalist would say that this is a classic example of a state husbanding its resources to advance state purposes and using its power to advance state goals. A lawyer would note that the federalist is advancing their goals *without* actively blocking the federal government from accomplishing its lawful and constitutional objectives.

In a way, these laws represented the blue-state alternative to a very different, red-state immigration vision articulated by Arizona just a few years before. In 2010, alarmed by the increase in illegal immigration in the state and the corresponding strain on social services, the state legislature passed a statute called the Support Our Law Enforcement and Safe Neighborhoods Act. The goal was "attrition [of illegal immigration] through enforcement." The law made it a state misdemeanor to fail to comply with federal alien registration requirements. It also made it a state misdemeanor for an illegal alien to seek or engage in work in the state. Further, it required officers who stopped, arrested, or detained individuals under specific circumstances to attempt to determine their immigration status. Finally, the law empowered officers to arrest a person who they had "probable cause to believe . . . has committed any public offense that makes the person removable from the United States."4

Arizona's law allocated state resources to *enhance* federal immigration enforcement efforts. California's law restricted the use of state resources in federal immigration enforcement so as to *inhibit* (without affirmatively interfering with) that enforcement. But neither law bound or restricted the actual operation of federal agents in any way.

That's classic federalism.

But the Obama administration sued to block Arizona's law, and the Trump administration sued to stop California. And each step of the way partisans took contradictory positions.

On June 25, 2012, the Supreme Court struck down the key provisions of the Arizona law. Justice Anthony Kennedy wrote the opinion, and it was sweeping in its language and scope. Essentially, Kennedy ruled that Congress—through its comprehensive statutory scheme—had "occupied the field" of alien registration and thus "even *complementary* state regulation is impermissible" (emphasis added). This "field preemption" reflects "a congressional decision to foreclose *any* state regulation in the area [preempted], even if it is parallel to federal standards."

After waxing eloquent about the importance of immigration in the American national story, Kennedy's opinion goes on to conclude that "Arizona may have understandable frustrations with the problems caused by illegal immigration . . . but the State may not pursue policies that undermine federal law." In other words, it wasn't just that federal law trumped state law, federal priorities (as embodied in law) trumped state priorities.

If Arizona's citizens wanted to do more to protect their communities from the negative effects of illegal immigration, well, too bad.

Justice Antonin Scalia wrote an opinion concurring in part and dissenting in part that surveyed relevant American constitutional history, discussed the nature of state sovereignty, and reached a conclusion that California would almost certainly like to cling to today:

> In light of the predominance of federal immigration restrictions in modern times, it is easy to lose sight of the States' traditional role in regulating immigration—and to overlook their sovereign prerogative to do so. I accept as a given that State regulation is excluded by the Constitution when (1) it has been prohibited by a valid federal law, or (2) it conflicts with federal regulation—when, for example, it admits those whom federal regulation would exclude, or excludes those whom federal regulation would admit.

Under the Kennedy framework, if Arizona's efforts at creating complementary policy were impermissible, then California faces an immense challenge justifying a policy that is quite explicitly designed to undermine federal enforcement.[5] According to Kennedy's reasoning (adopted by Justices John Roberts, Stephen Breyer, Ruth Bader Ginsburg, and Sonia Sotomayor), federal statutes are precisely designed to accomplish national goals—goals that no state can undermine.

Scalia's reasoning, firmly rooted in American constitutional tradition, represents federalism as the Founders intended. The Founders recognized that America wasn't a single sovereign entity but rather a unified nation comprising multiple distinct and different states with their own sovereign interests. The federal government is supreme, but in the absence of conflict with federal law, the states have considerable discretion to fashion their own policies. They are, after all, different in history, politics, geography, and culture.

But now? Federalism has become a tactic, not a principle. It's a defense mechanism when you're out of power and an annoyance when you're in power. Federalists are the losers of the last national election. Nationalists are the winners. Then, when the outcomes change, the identities change. That's why the Obama administration sued Arizona, and the Trump administration is suing California. That's why the same people who cheered the Obama administration's Supreme Court victory in 2012 will complain bitterly if the Trump administration wins its suit in the years to come. And that's why all too many conservatives who supported Arizona now want to bring down the hammer on California.

It will take more time and more pain before Americans on both sides (hopefully) remember the wisdom of the Founders and understand that centralized control of an ideologically diverse and polarized nation is not only elusive but destructive. Healthy federalism could temper polarization by empowering self-governance. Cynical, fake federalism divides us with its dishonesty.

Is there any hope at all for a way through this morass?

In 2018 *World* magazine's Marvin Olasky interviewed me for his podcast. The subject was national polarization, and I previewed for him many of the themes of this book. When we were discussing federalism, he asked a simple question: Why would either side give up the drive for domination? Why would either side be content with self-governance?

The answer, in the short run, is that a return to federalism is not on the table. The drive for domination is still too strong, and the hopes for domination are still high, but the probability of an impasse is too overwhelming for the hopes for domination to endure forever. The continued drift apart is too strong for meaningful hopes of moderate compromise. In that circumstance—and perhaps only in that circumstance—will partisan Americans begin to understand that the push for polarization combined with increased centralization creates unbearable downside risk.

In other words, as a progressive pundit told me in 2017, "I'm finally realizing that my vision of a centralized American system that embodies my values will never happen." But what can happen, if we're wise enough to embrace self-governance, is that we can live in communities that more closely mirror our values than if we continue to emphasize centralization. If we can actually let California be California and Tennessee be Tennessee, then we are highly likely not just to create communities that are more reflective of our values, but also to spend less time in a state of crisis—a posture of self-defense—that poisons our feelings for our fellow citizens.

But for Americans to embrace federalism as a concept, it just might take an issue—a cause that fires the imagination, a cause attainable only if our federal system loosens its grip.

It might take single-payer health care. And it just might take California to lead the way.

Could California Health Care Reform Revive American Federalism?

As I write this book, support for national single-payer health care—after rising sharply following Bernie Sanders's 2016 presidential campaign—seems to have peaked, at best. There does not seem to be a national appetite for what's often called "Medicare for All," a national program that would sweep away private insurance and place all Americans under a single government plan. The Republican Party is united against it, and Democrats are divided, with even some supporters reluctant to push it on a recalcitrant public.

But are the only options national single-payer or some version of the status quo? Or can health care reform at long last render federalism so attractive that progressives will take the lead in urging greater local control? Perhaps it's a pipe dream. It's probably a pipe dream, but if our nation's largest states could well be the instrument of American division, they can also be pioneers in a new American federalism.

On February 17, 2017, California state senators Ricardo Lara and Toni Atkins introduced the Healthy California Act, an extraordinarily ambitious plan to transform the health care industry in America's wealthiest and most populous state.[1] Like the "Medicare for All" plans put forth by Bernie Sanders and Elizabeth Warren, it proposed to do away with the hybrid public/private system dominated by Medicare, Medicaid, and private health insurance and replace it with the "Healthy California program," a "comprehensive universal single-payer health care coverage and a health care cost control system" designed to "incorporate the health care benefits and standards of other existing federal and state provisions, including, but not limited to, the state's Children's Health Insurance Program (CHIP), Medi-Cal, ancillary health care or social services covered by regional centers for persons with developmental disabilities, Knox-Keene, and the federal Medicare program."

Moreover, the bill "would prohibit health care service plans and health insurers from offering health benefits or covering any service for which coverage is offered to individuals under the program." In plain English, the senators proposed a state takeover of health care in California so comprehensive that it would actively *bar* most forms of competing, private insurance. As Sally Pipes, president of the Pacific Research Institute, summarized it in *Forbes*, "Public officials would determine which drugs, procedures, and services the one-size-fits-all system covers. Care would be free at the point of service. Californians would pay no premiums, deductibles, or co-pays, and referrals to specialists would not be necessary."[2]

The cost would be staggering, reaching a total of $400 billion—almost triple the state's annual budget. It would represent a government takeover of almost 20 percent of the state's economy, and it would represent a culture change as an entire state shed the health care system that dominates the rest of the nation.

In other words, the Healthy California Act is a radical piece of legislation—but not too radical to race through the California Senate. In April 2017 it passed the Health Committee by a 5–2 vote. In May it passed the Appropriations Committee, and in June the whole Senate voted to approve the boldest piece of legislation in all fifty states by a 23–14 margin.[3]

Then the proposed legislation moved into the California Assembly, where cooler heads prevailed. The bill died, but California's governor, Gavin Newsom, has long endorsed the concept and is committed both to expanding the government's role in health care and to presenting California as a national model of progressive governance. So the stage is still set for large-scale progressive experimentation in health care.

When I read about the California debate, I immediately shuddered. As a conservative, I want no part of single-payer health care, and if I lived in California, I'd contest it vigorously. I generally like my private health insurance, and I particularly like the range of choices available in the private market. As an American, however, I look at the debate and see something else—a perhaps once-in-a-decade opportunity to break apart the immense national government social welfare superstructure and empower a new era in state experimentation and a new era in American self-governance.

Why am I so intrigued? It's simple. For California to execute its plan, it would need to wrest away from the federal government control over the approximately $200 billion in health care funds that Californians send to

Washington in Medicare and Medicaid premiums and other expenses. It would also need to wrest away federal regulatory control of insurance coverage. In other words, California would have to virtually secede from the national health care safety net and reconstitute its own, more generous program. It simply could not create a single-payer program without a declaration of independence from the federal system—a declaration of independence that would have to be endorsed by the federal government.[4]

Now, while this declaration of independence would be necessary to fund single-payer health care in the state, it would not be sufficient. The remainder of the money would have to come through increased taxes on California taxpayers. There is a vigorous argument over whether these increased taxes would be offset by the decrease in overall health care expenses. In other words, would the savings on health insurance premiums, copays, deductibles, and other expenses (those would all zero out) compensate for the increased taxes?

But consider the precedent if California did seek congressional approval to break away from the federal health care leviathan. There is no constitutional issue with such a request. After all, there's no provision of the Constitution that grants the federal government exclusive jurisdiction over health care policy. The decision to permit California to go its own way would instead be one of the most consequential political, economic, and cultural decisions in modern American politics.

After all, if California seeks control of the funds it sends to Washington, what is to stop Tennessee from seeking its own waivers? What's to stop New York? Or

Alabama? In fact, given the extraordinarily disproportionate share of federal funds spent on health care, a
transfer of such funding back to the states would tip the
balance of total government funding away from the central government and back to states and localities. The
federal government would no longer be the dominant financial force in American fiscal life.

Even better, moving control of health care funding
back to the states would represent a form of federalism
that isn't just constitutionally acceptable, but would be
constitutionally *preferable*.

Consider the Founders' vision of American government—as modified by constitutional amendments (especially the Civil War amendments). They envisioned a
government of limited, specifically enumerated powers.
They perceived the primary role of the federal government as the preservation and protection of liberty. In
contrast with the federal government, the state governments possessed what is known as the "police power"—
the generalized power to regulate its citizens and pass
laws for the public welfare. In other words, the Founders
would be surprised that welfare programs like Medicare
are administered by the federal government. They would
see the regulation and provision of health services (to the
extent it was a government function at all) as a state responsibility. The system was built from the ground up to
accommodate this level of state authority.

But as the worst elements of our national history have
taught us, safeguards against the state's police power are
necessary. The Declaration of Independence's statement
that some rights are "unalienable" applies to every level
of government. The Bill of Rights protected our core,

unalienable rights from federal authority, but in the original framing of the Constitution, protecting unalienable rights from state encroachment was left to state constitutions.

In hindsight, the Founders placed too much trust in the states. Many states not only proved incapable of protecting individual liberty, they proved they could and would energetically suppress the exercise of the most basic rights, including the right to free speech. The Civil War amendments were intended in many ways to close this loophole, to guarantee protection of the "privileges and immunities" of citizenship even from the power of state and local governments.

Thus, healthy federalism grants wide authority to the states to regulate health care, fashion environmental policy, create economic incentives, and establish pension plans—to do all the things that governments do (aside from those functions that are reserved to the federal government or that conflict with federal authority). Healthy federalism does *not*, however, grant states the power to restrict individual liberty more than the Bill of Rights allows. No matter where they live, all citizens should enjoy a certain minimum level of guaranteed rights. States can grant more liberty than required by the Bill of Rights, but they cannot grant less.

To better understand the distinctions, let's turn our attention back again to—where else?—the state of California.

Federalism Ends Where the Bill of Rights Begins

Early in 2018, conservative social media briefly lit up with news of yet another California progressive excess. The state's Democratic house majority leader submitted a bill that imposed *criminal penalties* on restaurants that offered their customers plastic straws. Yes, you read that correctly. Here's the description, from the legislative counsel's digest:

> This bill would prohibit a full-service restaurant, as specified, from providing single-use plastic straws, as defined, to consumers unless requested by the consumer. The bill would specify that the first and 2nd violations of these provisions would result in a notice of violation and any subsequent violation would be an infraction punishable by a fine of $25 for each day the full-service restaurant is in violation, but not to exceed an annual total of $300. The provisions would be enforced by the same officers authorized to enforce the California Retail Food Code. By creating a new crime and imposing additional

enforcement duties on local health agencies, this bill would impose a state-mandated local program.[1]

Conservatives couldn't believe their eyes. A bill criminalizing the dispensing of straws? Is there a worse example of malignant nannyism in all the United States? Incredibly, the bill passed. It sailed through the Assembly. It sailed through the Senate. And on September 20, 2018, the governor of California, Jerry Brown, signed it into law.

It's not worth spending too much time on this absurd bill (and I do mean absurd—*Reason* magazine investigated the arguments for the bill and found that the support for it rests on significantly flawed research conducted by a nine-year-old).[2] Still, it's a useful segue to a far more significant point. California is presently in the midst of an experiment in progressive governance and active resistance that is combining to create a simultaneously dangerous *and* tantalizing experiment in state autonomy.

By early 2019, the state government had filed no fewer than forty-six separate lawsuits against the Trump administration. That represented almost two complaints per month for the first two years of Trump's first term, with challenges touching at least seventeen different subject areas.[3]

Moreover, as discussed at length earlier, California is considering radical health care reforms, and it is now a "sanctuary state" and therefore sharply limits the extent to which its citizens or public entities can voluntarily cooperate with federal immigration authorities. Its commitment to immigration is so extreme that it even considered imposing penalties on companies that worked to build a Trump border wall.

In response to President Trump's decision to pull the United States from the Paris climate accords, California led a coalition of cities and states that vowed to keep American commitments all on their own. This vow supplements its own unique and comprehensive environmental policy. It has also created its own version of a sanctions regime by imposing travel bans on state-funded travel to states that California deems insufficiently LGBT-friendly.

While I'd fight similar measures were they to come up for a vote in Tennessee, they represent proper examples of federalism in action. A progressive state has a right to implement progressive policies.

But California goes too far. It's one thing to implement a unique health care plan or create comprehensive environmental regulations. It's another thing entirely to try to opt out of the Bill of Rights. In 2017 and 2018, California attempted to implement and enforce a confiscation program for high-capacity magazines, an act that directly implicates the Second Amendment,[4] and it went to the Supreme Court of the United States in an unsuccessful attempt to require pro-life pregnancy centers to advertise that the state will fund free or low-cost abortions, an attempt to compel speech that violated the First Amendment.[5]

At the same time, only a veto by Governor Brown prevented the state from violating the First Amendment again by requiring a faith-based organization to hire individuals who disagreed with its stance on abortion and sexual morality. The measure would have injected the state directly into the hiring and firing decisions of religious organizations.

Similarly, the state almost passed a bill that would have declared "sexual orientation change efforts" to be an "unlawful business practice." Initially the bill was so broadly and poorly written that it encompassed even the sale of books if those books advocated for a change in sexual behavior. As amended, it still prohibited any individuals from selling "services" that advocated a change in sexual behavior—a direct attack on the First Amendment rights of those who would argue for traditional Jewish, Christian, or Muslim positions on sexual morality.

California can and should—if it wishes—secede from the federal regulatory leviathan. It can and should go its own way on health care, environmental regulations, and economic policy. It can build its own bureaucracy, and it shouldn't have to actively cooperate with federal law enforcement priorities. If the federal government wants to enforce federal law, it can do so with federal resources. So long as the state doesn't actively impede the enforcement of constitutionally valid laws, there is no constitutional problem with sanctuary cities or sanctuary states. That's federalism.

But no, California, cannot secede from the Bill of Rights. It cannot secede from the Constitution. It cannot "abridge the privileges or immunities of citizens of the United States." In other words, California, craft your own environmental policy, but leave the First Amendment alone. Design your own health care system, but preserve religious liberty.

To grant state authority at the expense of the fundamental privileges and immunities of American citizenship is to repeat the grave American error that led to the Civil War, perpetuated Jim Crow, and oppressed marginalized communities throughout American history. A state that rejects the Bill of Rights imposes second-class-citizen status on the targets of its unconstitutional ire. I don't suffer an injury to my fundamental rights if I'm denied access to plastic straws, required to drive a more fuel-efficient car, or forced to obtain government health care. I am deprived of my fundamental rights if that state squelches my ability to practice my faith, speak about my deepest beliefs, or enjoy the most basic rights of due process. Breaching the Bill of Rights breaks the compact between citizen and state.

Moreover, California progressives must understand that the desire for autonomy goes both ways. After the 2018 election, the short era of Republican dominance of all the elected branches of the federal government ended. The pendulum may swing further toward the Democrats in 2020. If and when it does—whether it's 2020, 2024, or some later time—will they preserve for conservative states the same autonomy they coveted during the days of GOP ascendance, or does respect for federalism exist only when it protects them?

Federalism is so simple. It has profound appeals. It permits progressives to build progressive communities. It permits conservatives to build conservative communities. At the same time, as the federal government protects the unalienable rights of all citizens, neither progressive nor conservative states can go so far as to oppress dissenters. They cannot squelch opposition. They cannot stifle religious practice. They cannot deprive individuals of due process, the right to counsel, or the right to be free of cruel and unusual punishment. In other words, healthy federalism is a system of protected customization. To borrow a term from campus, it carves out a constitutional "safe space" for distinctive regions and distinctive cultures.

Properly executed, it avoids the destabilizing problem articulated in Part I of this book, even as we would continue to live in states that are geographically contiguous and enjoy distinct cultures. The citizens of those states would not fear that their way of life is under threat. Much less would that fear escalate into life-or-death alarm.

Simply put, the most significant government decisions, aside from the decision to go to war, shouldn't be made by the government entity most distant from your life. This is why the American in me who is concerned for the unity and health of our constitutional republic *wants* to see California try single-payer. The part of me that is tired of an overreaching federal government (even when I agree with its policy aims) is glad that California is telling the federal government to enforce its own laws.

But that satisfaction applies only if those precedents apply to red states and blue states alike. I would like to see greater state-level conservative experimentation in health care and social welfare. And when a progressive federal government tries to impose its priorities on a conservative state, its governor and legislature should be able to tell the feds to keep to their own work.

And this is exactly where my optimism falters. Federalism as applied in the United States is still mainly just a tactic, not a bedrock principle of governance, and state experimentation is often not a precedent for greater variation but a test run for nationalization—even for nationalization imposed by a straight partisan vote.

Obamacare is the perfect example of federalism as practice for nationalization. Progressives are right that it is based in large part on a bipartisan state experiment—what was dubbed "Romneycare" in Massachusetts. In that state, Governor Mitt Romney (a Republican) worked with a Democratic-dominated state legislature and passed health care reform that contained many of the same central features of Obamacare. Importantly, by the time Obamacare was considered, Romneycare—though not perfect—was achieving its central goal of decreasing the number of uninsured residents in the state. Affordable health insurance was in reach for the vast majority of Massachusetts citizens.

So, time to take it national, right? If federalism is the "laboratory of democracy," then the individual mandate had passed its lab test, right?

Well, that was the argument, and it was a bad one. If you know anything from this book, you know that American states are not all alike. They have different economies. They have different cultures. If Romneycare was working in Massachusetts (a hotly debated contention in 2008, by the way), then the next prudent move might have been to try it in a different state. Or perhaps a few different states, with state legislatures crafting distinct statutory schemes to meet their respective populations' distinct needs.

Take, for example, the vast differences in wealth and rates of uninsurance between Massachusetts and our nation's poorer states. At the time, Massachusetts was our third-wealthiest state. Even before state-level health care reform, it had the lowest percentage of uninsured citizens in the nation.[6] To close the gap, to get as close to 100 percent coverage as possible, was a far less challenging prospect there than in poorer states, where up to 24 percent of the population had no health insurance.

Moreover, there was a process difference between Romneycare and Obamacare. Romney turned his attention to health care only after balancing the state budget, and his reform passed with broad bipartisan support. Obamacare was passed in a time of record deficits and—critically—was the first major piece of social reform legislation rammed through on a straight party-line vote in the history of the United States.

Is it a coincidence that this moment marked the beginning of a sharp escalation in conservative polarization against Democrats? The raw exercise of power—especially on matters of immense import—always alienates. It always polarizes. And when that raw exercise of power occurs at a national scale, it leaves dissenting Americans without options. A move from state to state won't allow them to escape national regulatory regimes. A move from state to state won't protect them if it is the *federal* government limiting their rights.

California single-payer, to take the principal example of this section of the book, could help ease American polarization if it breaks the cycle of increased federal uniformity and empowers an age of distinctive experimentation and a return of greater power to state and local governments. Or, if the present lack of commitment to true federalism holds, it could help break America if its adoption in one state is used as the justification for nationalization against the will of a critical mass of American citizens, especially if that critical mass lives in our geographically contiguous, culturally distinct zones of particular polarization.

This is the promise and appeal of federalism at its most compelling. It represents the vision of the Founders.

It lowers the stakes of national politics. It allows your vote to count and removes the sense of helplessness and distant alienation that all too many of us feel when we know that decisions that profoundly affect our lives are being made by the people who are most alien to us, most removed from our communities and our culture.

But I don't quite yet trust that Americans fully understand that promise. Too many of us can't quite give up the will to power or the quest to dominate. One of the most pernicious effects of negative polarization is that if we truly are Republican or Democratic less because of the strength of our own ideas and more because of hatred or fear of the other side, then for too many millions of Americans, defeating the ideological enemy and frustrating their ideological ambitions is far more politically satisfying even than building a local or state community that embodies and advances your own political values.

In fact, if one examines emerging intellectual trends in American conservatism, you'll see that the right is moving in exactly the opposite direction necessary to accommodate American pluralism and foster national reconciliation. The contemporary right-wing project of so-called national conservatism doubles down on centralized government power while weakening the modern conservative commitment to individual liberty.

Think of the controversy that ignited months of conservative debate in 2019. A New York–based right-wing writer was so infuriated by the thought of a drag queen story hour taking place in a library on the opposite side of the continent—in Sacramento, California—that he used the fact of the scheduled story hour to declare that my commitment to pluralism was inadequate to meet the challenge of the times. And what was his "solution" that would end the existence of a vanishingly small number of drag queen story hours at a few dozen libraries across the land? In a debate he declared an intention to undermine generations of First Amendment jurisprudence and grant the government the ability to exclude private citizens from using public facilities if the government dislikes those citizens' constitutionally protected speech.

And while that was but one proposal from one public intellectual, prominent right-wing political figures are proposing using the power of of the government to unconstitutionally regulate political speech. In June 2019 Missouri senator Josh Hawley rolled out a proposed bill called the Ending Support for Internet Censorship Act.[7] The bill would require large social media companies to obtain a certification from the government that they "[do] not moderate information provided by other information content providers in a manner that is biased against a political party, political candidate, or political viewpoint" before they could enjoy the benefits of Section 230 of the Communications Decency Act.

Section 230 permits internet companies to moderate or exclude from their virtual pages material that they consider to be "obscene, lewd, lascivious, filthy, excessively violent, harassing, or otherwise objectionable" without being deemed a "publisher" of its users' content for purposes of defamation law. This is what allows Instagram and Facebook to remove porn from their pages, or Twitter to remove virulent racist slurs, without rendering them liable for the contents of users' posts. But this law also grants companies the ability to moderate content in accordance

with corporate values—to discriminate against the kinds
of speech they find particularly distasteful.

While the possibility of politically biased moderation
is obvious, Section 230 is and remains the statutory foundation of free speech on the internet. It's what allows you
to post a Yelp review, to comment on a news story, or to
participate in a Facebook conversation without facing a
potential corporate screening process that would dramatically limit your public voice. If companies become liable
for your speech online, many of them will be unlikely to
risk letting you speak at all. Celebrities, journalists, and
politicians will retain their platforms. They don't need
social media to reach the public. You will find yourself
silenced across the length and breadth of the internet.

Hawley's proposal—designed in response to a few
high-profile complaints about bias by Facebook, Twitter,
YouTube, and Google—would place the government in
charge of defining and enforcing "neutrality" in a way
that's alien to American constitutional law. His proposed
legislation even goes so far as to place the government in
charge of regulating not just the language of social media
speech policies, but also their intent and effect.

Think of the impact on national politics. Each presidential race, candidates would be running not just to
control the executive branch of the federal government,
but also to control the political speech policies of every
popular social media app on your phone. At a time when
America desperately needs to decentralize government
authority and deescalate national politics, Hawley's proposal would consolidate national power and increase the
stakes of presidential elections.

For the foreseeable future, the cycle of misery will continue, and the cynical misuse of federalism will endure. We'll do this time and again until Americans reembrace local control or until our union finally starts to fracture. California's soft secession can be promising or perilous. The conservative turn toward nationalism promises to foster even greater divisiveness. No one doubts that our states are different. No one doubts that in many ways those differences are increasing. It's how we handle that diversity that will decide our nation's fate.

A Call for Courage

So, is there hope for tolerance to break out? Can we re-create a national political culture that values the voluntary associations of civil society and the self-governance and community autonomy of federalism? Will cultural antibodies emerge to save the body politic from the disease of negative polarization? Frankly, I'm not optimistic. In part it's because the tolerance that's indispensable to pluralism requires a degree of political and moral courage, and in modern America that kind of courage is in short supply.

Allow me to relate two personal anecdotes—one on the left and one on the right—that sum up the extent to which fear grips even the most powerful members of the American elite. Not long ago I had a candid conversation with a progressive professor at one of America's most elite universities, an upper-tier Ivy. His progressive credentials were impeccable—he was formerly a senior adviser to a Democratic presidential candidate and had spent much of his life in Democratic politics—and his job security was near-absolute. It's extraordinarily difficult to fire a tenured professor in the Ivy League.

While he and I seek very different policy outcomes, we both consider ourselves classical liberals dedicated to the American constitutional order. We both value free speech, due process, and the rest of the core protections in the Bill of Rights (though we differ strongly about the Second Amendment), and he was deeply troubled by the intolerance he witnessed on his own campus. He told me stories of students who attempted to bully peers and professors alike, and he made a confession.

"I'm terrified of my own students," he said. And while actual terror was inappropriate, there was no reason to doubt that his students could make his life miserable. Even if they could not truly take his job, accusations of racism and sexism could stain him in the eyes of his colleagues and harm his professional reputation. Frivolous Title IX claims could drain his financial resources. The sheer fury of the attack would take its emotional toll.

Even worse, he knew that he'd have to face any such ordeal largely alone. Other professors would see the misery he was enduring and choose to remain silent. Yes, there might be scattered help here and there—and an occasional essay or tweet thread in his defense—but he knew beyond a shadow of a doubt that the number of colleagues who condemned him would almost certainly outnumber the number who supported him, and the rest of his peers would remain mute, afraid to lift a finger to aid a friend in need.

So he remained silent, and in remaining silent he permits the intolerant and illiberal wing of the left to dominate his campus and exert outsized influence on his community.

At the same time, fear grips part of the right. In D.C. circles, it's well known that Republican politicians and activists will often say things they don't truly believe during television and media appearances, for fear that if they share their true feelings and criticize the president, then they'll risk perhaps their public office (to primary challengers) or their careers (when facing angry donors). So they lie. Or they don't tell the whole truth. And by feeding the audience the information they want to hear, they perversely feed the very beast that threatens to devour them.

Moreover, this fear grips even religious leaders. I've sat in the same room with pastors, professors, and leaders of religious colleges who consistently say the exact same thing: they must be very careful about disclosing what they truly believe, lest they enrage the congregation, alienate donors, or trigger a wave of controversy that will swamp the rest of their ministry.

Even worse, the rise of the alt-right and other right-wing online mobs means that critics of the Trump administration often face consequences much more serious than "mere" social sanction or threats to their careers. They often face direct, malicious harassment that threatens their very lives.

At the beginning of this book I briefly told the story of the harassment my family suffered. I said that I was not alone. To this day, Americans do not appreciate the sheer scale of the harassment and threats directed at Trump critics. They do not appreciate that the price of opposing the Republican president could include the very real fear that your family—including your children—could face direct reprisals.

Yes, the threats came from a fringe, but an active fringe can reach a wide number of people, and soon enough every person with any public platform understands that each act of dissent from the party line risks a response unlike any they've previously encountered in public life.

Yet I've come to believe that while fear and silence in the face of threats and intimidation are understandable, they are ultimately not *justifiable*. Maintaining America's constitutional order requires courage. The maintenance of civil society cannot be delegated entirely to the government. In fact, there is no satisfactory solution to the challenge of negative polarization absent courage and character, including a renewed commitment to courage and character on the part of our national leadership.

In past times of national crisis, time and again there has emerged a generation of leaders who have transcended the partisan pettiness and vindictiveness that have always been a part of the human condition. While politics is downstream from culture, and thus culture shapes politics far more than politics shapes culture, in key times great leaders have stepped forward to not just guide the nation, but shape it in a particular image.

But it's never just one leader. At critical times those leaders have been supported by a coalition of wise men and women. The Founding generation is a prime example. George Washington was indispensable, but so was John Adams. So was Thomas Jefferson. So was James Madison. So was Alexander Hamilton. It is remarkable to think how decisively history was shaped by a relatively small group of wise individuals who were providentially gathered on the same strip of colonies on the same coast at the same time.

While we rightly extol Abraham Lincoln, never forget that for all his resolve, wisdom, and charity, he was a failing wartime leader until he found the generals who could win the war. Lincoln would likely be remembered quite differently without Grant and Sherman. And would abolition have succeeded when it did without the fire of Frederick Douglass, the courage and example of Harriet Tubman, or the words of Harriet Beecher Stowe?

And it's easy to forget that there is a reason Americans before Vietnam had developed an immense amount of trust in the national political establishment. It wasn't just Roosevelt who guided America through World War II. There was a generation of leaders who devised a war-winning strategy and then constructed the framework of the Cold War strategy that ultimately defeated the Soviet Union without a third devastating conflict in the twentieth century—while at the same time helping our nation become an economic colossus.

Moreover, we can also know the power of a transformative political class when we feel its absence. How much did our nation miss the wisdom and resolve of Abraham Lincoln when Civil War triumph turned into a botched Reconstruction followed by the darkness of Jim Crow?

There are good reasons distrust of institutions is on the rise. It is *earned* distrust. Time and again politicians, academics, and members of the press have been caught being dishonest, incompetent, and/or corrupt. Yes, some of the criticism has been unfair, and not even our best leaders are perfect, but is anyone willing to argue that the present generation of American political leaders and cultural elites is ready to stand in the shoes of the best generations that came before?

At best, our national elite is hostage to larger forces— along for the ride as tectonic changes in technology, culture, and faith drive changes they can scarcely understand, much less manage.

At worst, that same national elite is doing its best to drive the bus of division. There is no anguished choice between truth and tribe. The truth was never an option. When push comes to shove, they place self-interest and partisan interest over even the most basic of virtues.

At present, there is simply too much money to make and too much power to gain to think twice about punching your enemy as hard as you can. That's when you hear the roar of the crowds. As a son of the conservative movement, I've seen this impulse slowly begin to dominate the right as cultural and economic incentives align to time and again grant the most fame and fortune to those who stoke the most rage.

For example, it's hard to overstate the power of Fox News for those seeking a career in the conservative movement. I've seen the most accomplished of lawyers suddenly become "somebody" only *after* they began regularly appearing on Fox. I've seen young activists leave senators or representatives languishing alone at conferences as they flood over to Fox personalities, seeking selfies. Fox has become the prime gatekeeper of conservative fame, the source of conservative book deals, and the ticket into the true pantheon of conservative influence.

At any given moment Fox may have the biggest audience in cable news, but its overall cultural and political influence is less than that of its leading network and internet competitors. Fox has constructed a big, beautiful, and lucrative gated community—a comfortable conservative cocoon.[1]

The result is plain: Conservatives gain fame, power,

and influence mainly by talking to each other. They persuade each other of the rightness of their ideas and write Fox-fueled bestselling books making arguments that Fox viewers love. The sheer size of the audience lulls minor political celebrities into believing that they're making a cultural and political difference. But they never get a chance to preach to the unconverted.

The problem goes well beyond this cocoon effect, into the very moral and intellectual heart of the conservative movement. Like any human enterprise, Fox is filled with a wide variety of people—some good, some bad. But it is, at heart, a *commercial* endeavor, rather than an intellectual or spiritual one. Its fundamental priority is to make money, not to advance a particular set of ideas or values in public life.

To be clear, one of the ways that it makes money is through a very deliberate strategy of counterprogramming the mainstream media. But that is an economic determination far more than an ideological one. It's based on eyeballs, not ideas. But the quest for eyeballs transforms the perception of ideas.

Such is the power of Fox fame that I've seen with my own eyes conservative leaders alter their message and public priorities in response to Fox's demands. "Fox isn't interested" is a statement that often shuts down conversations and ends public campaigns before they begin. On the other hand, if Fox *is* interested, the conversation never ends. Ever wonder why conservatives talk so much about Benghazi almost four full years after the vast majority of the key facts of that tragic engagement became clear? Because Fox remains interested.

The result is a world in which many individual conservatives just keep failing up. Fox is the place where you can nurse grievances over failed arguments. It's the place where you can make money after failed campaigns. Do you wonder why the GOP had seventeen presidential primary candidates in 2016? In part it's because there were actually two primary contests—the race for the nomination and the auditions for Fox.

But lest those on the left sneer at conservatives for their unique dysfunction, we cannot forget that the progressive movement's cultural enclaves have had their own profound challenges. The drumbeat of revelations from the #MeToo movement caught places like Fox, yes, but they also swept through the entertainment industry, shaking it to its core and demonstrating to anyone with eyes to see that adopting progressive politics is no guarantee of personal virtue.

I've already discussed in some detail the challenges to individual liberty on college campuses, but I've seen firsthand as a student and teacher at two different Ivy League universities the dreary ideological monoculture and the vicious hostility to dissent. Fox is far more ideologically diverse than, for example, the humanities faculty at virtually any academic institution of note. There are now men and women who spend their entire careers in academia without encountering a single socially conservative colleague.

Entire swaths of American culture aren't just underrepresented in the American academy, they're often unknown in the professional academic class. Many professors experience red America solely through their sometimes contentious encounters with much younger and less-educated conservative students. These mismatches only serve to reinforce a bulletproof sense of cultural and intellectual superiority.

There is a better way.

My *Dispatch* colleague Jonah Goldberg named his popular podcast *The Remnant*—a name so good that I'm still angry he thought of it first. It stands for the position he's staked out within the conservative movement as part of a remnant of people who did not ally themselves with President Trump and remained devoted not just to conservative policies (policies the president sometimes advances) but also to conservative cultural values, including the immense importance of personal character in public life.

It's a name with a rich theological heritage, harking back to Elijah's lament to God in the time when the false god Baal dominated Israelite life and Elijah feared the sword of the king. In an encounter with God, Elijah declared himself to be "the only one left" in service to the Lord. But God contradicted him, declaring that he had reserved "seven thousand in Israel—all whose knees have not bowed down to Baal and whose mouths have not kissed him."

Time and time again in biblical history the people of God are reduced to nothing but the smallest of remnants. How many people followed Jesus to the foot of the cross? Even after the Resurrection, the Book of Acts describes the sum total of believers as numbering around 120.

The word "remnant" carries with it the unmistakable pain of loss. It's the surviving portion of the larger whole. But, critically, the remnant also represents the seed of renewal.

The seven thousand who did not bend the knee to Baal represented the core of a Jewish faith that thrives still today, with adherents numbering in the tens of millions. The tiny number who wept at the foot of the cross were the human seed for the billions of Christians who would live in the generations to come. The remnant is the shattered remains of a larger movement, but it is also the hope for a brighter future to come.

In that sense, the call to action in this book is not just a call for cultural or political change—though greater tolerance and more federalism would go a long way toward easing our national polarization. It's also a call to model the values of the generations that built and sustained our nation for more than two centuries.

It's increasingly clear now that there are two culture wars in American life. Yes, there is the right/left culture war that we're long familiar with, but there's now an even deeper struggle—between decency and indecency.

There's the classic conservative/progressive split—the battle of pro-life versus pro-choice or of single-payer versus market-based health care reforms. This fight rages, and it will continue to rage for the foreseeable future. The second front, however, is between those people of all political persuasions who continue to believe in constitutional processes and basic democratic norms, on the one hand, and those people who've adopted the anything-goes, end-justifies-the-means tactics of the campus social justice warrior or the "Flight 93" Trump populist, on the other.

Our nation is built from the ground up to handle political disagreement. It is not built to endure mass-scale dishonesty and vindictiveness. No less a light than John Adams understood our nation's unique vulnerability to individual depravity. In his October 11, 1798, letter to the Massachusetts Militia, Adams famously wrote that "our Constitution was made only for a moral and religious People. It is wholly inadequate to the government of any other."

But that sentence doesn't quite capture the essence of his argument. He's talking not just about personal morality, but also about a distinct form of political virtue. Here's the core of Adams's letter:

> While our Country remains untainted with the Principles and manners, which are now producing desolation in so many Parts of the World: while she continues Sincere and incapable of insidious and impious Policy: We shall have the Strongest Reason to rejoice in the local destination assigned Us by Providence. But should the People of America, once become capable of that deep simulation towards one another and towards foreign nations, which assumes the Language of Justice and moderation while it is practicing Iniquity and Extravagance; and displays in the most captivating manner the charming Pictures of Candour frankness & sincerity while it is rioting in rapine and Insolence: this Country will be the most miserable Habitation in the World. Because We have no Government armed with Power capable of contending with human Passions unbridled by morality and Religion. Avarice, Ambition [and] Revenge or Galantry, would break the strongest Cords of our Constitution as a Whale goes through a Net.

Is there any better description of the culture of negative polarization than two sides assuming "the language of justice and moderation" while "practicing iniquity and extravagance"? Do we not have a political culture consumed with avarice, ambition, and—significantly—revenge? The final image, of breaking the cords of our Constitution "as a Whale goes through a Net," is a fitting symbol of the fragility of political culture beset by viciousness and vice.

So, what does this mean for you? Quite simply, it means that you must be prepared to lead. If a nation wearies of intolerance and spite, be prepared to model tolerance and grace even as you keep to your underlying principles and convictions. If a nation wearies of centralization and uniformity, a new leadership should be prepared to show what it means to surrender the will to power sufficiently to allow distinct communities to build local governments in their distinct cultural images.

This is not a call for political moderation. The call for moderation is ultimately no different from calling for an end to conflict through the triumph of conservatism or liberalism. Of course political divisions would ease if Americans reached political agreement under any ideological banner. But, barring an unforeseen transformation, political agreement is not on the horizon. Even consensus on one issue merely shifts the confrontation to another policy or proposal.

It is an enduring truth of virtually any sphere of life—from politics to sports to entertainment—that the people who care the most set the tone. Why do celebrities try so assiduously to court comic book fans when cast as the latest superhero? Because they know that the energy and enthusiasm of the committed few can win over the larger whole. Why do politicians sometimes spend months shaking hands with party activists across the length and breadth of their states and districts? Again, the committed few win over the larger whole.

For too long in American politics, the committed few have been disproportionately drawn from the ranks of the angriest and most vindictive Americans. The people who truly drive American political polarization represent a small slice of the overall population, but they set the tone for national political discourse. So it's easy to look at our polarized and decaying political elite and despair. If they set the tone, the future looks bleak. They're exacerbating, not mitigating, the political effects of larger national trends that pull Americans apart.

There is a need for a better American political class. But for now, there is little apparent demand. Those who care the most often hate the most, and one of their chief methods of discrediting ideological allies with whom they compete is by portraying them as too tolerant of the hated political enemy. Kindness is perceived as weakness. Decency is treated as if it's cowardice. Acts of grace are an unthinkable concession to evil.

But here's a simple, fundamental reality. If we are to manage our divisions with any kind of wisdom and foresight, that challenge is going to require a degree of decency and grace that is, sad to say, all too rare. It's going to require a distinctly American patriotism.

In the age of Trump, there's been much commentary and debate about the difference between patriotism and nationalism. There's been discussion about whether there is something unique about American patriotism, as distinct from the patriotism or nationalism that citizens of other countries feel for their own soil.

I think the answer is yes. There is something distinct about American patriotism. The best sort of American patriotism understands twin interlocking truths that were articulated by two Founding Fathers who were often fierce rivals, Thomas Jefferson and John Adams.

The first truth is encapsulated in some of the most famous words in the English language: "We hold these truths to be self-evident, that all men are created equal, that they are endowed by their Creator with certain unalienable Rights, that among these are Life, Liberty and the pursuit of Happiness." According to this founding principle, government exists for the very purpose of securing these rights.

This truth made manifest in our constitutional republic is the heart of the American idea. It represents the notion that our shared liberty binds us together more surely than soil or blood. Indeed, if we rely on soil or blood to bind us together, our union quickly starts to fray in the face of two questions most nations (far more homogenous than ours) don't have to answer.

Whose blood? Which soil?

When your nation spans a continent, a sense of collective place is harder to share. When your nation contains multitudes of virtually every race, creed, and color on planet Earth, a sense of shared blood is nonexistent. But men and women of dramatically different heritages and from fundamentally different places can and do unite around a shared idea—that each of us enjoys liberties so essential that our government is legitimate if and only if it guarantees their protection.

But organizing a nation around liberty brings with it a hidden danger, the danger of indulgence—the danger that a nation that protects the rights of the individual will become excessively individualistic, fracturing the bonds of community. And that brings us to the second essential truth of the American founding (and thus of American patriotism), the very words I just quoted from John Adams: "Our Constitution was made only for a moral and religious People. It is wholly inadequate to the government of any other."

The patriotic citizen understands that their liberty is governed and ordered by a higher purpose. We live not for ourselves. We are free, but we should view ourselves as free to pursue what is good and true, to *live* what is good and true.[2]

That's but one reason the spirit of our modern politics—excusing vice in the pursuit of alleged political virtue—is so toxic to our founding principles. Conservatives could succeed in jamming government back in its box, and we could thoroughly and completely defeat political correctness and identity politics, but if the people who live in that new atmosphere of freedom are consumed with "iniquity and extravagance," then we will live—as Adams warns—in the "most miserable Habitation in the world."

Similarly, committed progressives could triumph time and again in battles over everything from gender identity to health care, but "iniquity and extravagance" can immiserate a nation dedicated to social justice every bit as much as it can corrupt a nation dedicated to individual liberty.

It's a sad fact of our modern era that our warring factions spend an enormous amount of time battling over whether the government is upholding its end of the social compact. We spend less time looking inward, pondering how we exercise our blood-bought freedoms. In other words, we debate whether our nation is worthy of our patriotism. We simply assume we're worthy patriots.

We rarely turn reflective. We rarely spend serious time questioning our own role in making politics toxic or our indifference to cultural repair. But now is exactly the time to examine ourselves.

I reflect on these matters most on days like Memorial Day. I see the rows of flags by the gravestones. I think of my friends who fell during my deployment to Iraq. I hear the mournful bagpipes playing "Amazing Grace." And I'm reminded of the eternal truth that greater love has no man than when he lays down his life for his friends. The men and women in those graves laid down their lives for friends, for family, for citizens they'd never meet, and for generations to come.

In the presence of that greater love, the least I can do is to commit to show a more ordinary love, a love that asks us to live with decency and honor. It's a love that asks us to fulfill the purpose of humankind as articulated in Micah 6:8—to do justice, to love mercy, and to walk humbly with God.

I would suggest that there is no solution to our national crisis absent those three cardinal virtues. It's easy in polarized times to seek justice. After all, we fight our political, cultural, and religious battles because we think we are right. We believe we stand on the side of the angels, and our opponents are misguided. We justify the intensity of our passion by the conviction of the rightness of our cause.

But that's not the entirety of our commitment, of course. The next two qualities, mercy and humility, are indispensable to our national life. Mercy is the quality we display when we are, in fact, right and our opponents are wrong. We treat them not with contempt but with compassion. In the aftermath of political victory, we seek reconciliation. We operate with "malice towards none."

Humility reminds us that we are not perfect. Indeed, we are often wrong and will ourselves need mercy. As the apostle Paul reminds us, we "know in part." "We see through a glass darkly." Especially when tackling immense and complex challenges, we should face the task with resolve, but also with open hearts—ready to receive and hear criticism.

No matter the depth of our national division, there is no point where it is too late to show those virtues. There is no point where it is too risky to show those virtues. You can be despised for showing mercy and scorned for your humility, but national misery can last for only so long before the people cry out for a better way. We hope and pray that the cry for a better way comes before our national bonds are irretrievably broken.

But if the cry comes too late, even our wisest citizens may well reach a terrible conclusion—that our hate is too great and that separation, with all its pain and anguish, is preferable to continued union with a people you fear. We can hope that day will never come, but one thing is certain—we cannot simply presume our national unity will last.

ACKNOWLEDGMENTS

If you like this book at all, here's the people you need to thank—Adam Bellow, Kevin Reilly, and Alan Bradshaw. Adam saw the early drafts, read them carefully, and told me to get back to work. He was right. Kevin and Alan carried the ball across the goal line, and the final product is infinitely better because of their expertise and oversight. If you don't like the book? Well, that's on me.

Also, there are not many authors who can say that their agent was also the best man at their wedding. D. J. Snell is my friend and my business partner, and without him spurring me to write, I wouldn't put virtual pen to virtual paper.

I dedicated this book to my wife, Nancy, but she deserves more words than the short sentence at the start of the book. She's not just my best friend and the best possible mother. She's fiercely independent and dedicated to truth and justice. We've walked a difficult path since 2016, and she hasn't wavered—not for a moment—even in the face of terrifying threats.

I also want to thank my colleagues at *The Dispatch*, especially my good friends Steve Hayes and Jonah Goldberg. Their intellectual independence and moral courage are inspiring and give hope to our readers. But there are many others who demonstrate moral courage in this polarized time, including my progressive friends who've reached out to conservatives in the quest to build bridges.

Finally, I want to thank those who've read my work and listened to my podcasts. I'm honored beyond words that anyone actually cares what I think, and I'm so grateful for the words of encouragement and support (along with the words of thoughtful critique) that inspire me and instruct me as we try to navigate a difficult and perilous cultural and political landscape. Without you, this book would not exist. Thank you.

Introduction

1. Michael Anton (writing as "Publius Decius Mus"), *Claremont Review of Books*, September 5, 2016.

2. Definition taken from Patrick Deneen, *Why Liberalism Failed* (New Haven: Yale University Press, 2018).

3. Sohrab Ahmari, "Against David French-ism," *First Things*, May 29, 2019.

4. Frederick Douglass, "Plea for Free Speech in Boston," June 8, 1860, https://frederickdouglass.infoset.io/islandora/object/islandora:2129#page/1/mode/1up.

Chapter 1: Understanding the Geography of American Division

1. Gregor Aisch, Adam Pearce, and Karen Yourish, "The Divide Between Red and Blue America Grew Even Deeper in 2016," *New York Times*, November 10, 2016.

2. Ibid.

3. Niraj Chokshi, "Map: The Most Religious States in America," *Washington Post*, February 18, 2015.

4. For a general description of the economic power of each state, see Jeff Desjardins, "How Each US State's Economy Measures Up to Countries Around the World," *Business Insider*, June 2, 2018. For a more comprehensive chart, see Mark J. Perry, "Putting America's Enormous $19.4 Trillion Economy in Perspective by Comparing US State GDPs to Entire Countries," American Enterprise Institute, May 8, 2018.

5. You can find gun ownership rates here: http://demographicdata.org/facts-and-figures/gun-ownership-statistics; and church attendance rates here: https://news.gallup.com/poll/181601/frequent-church-attendance-highest-utah-lowest-vermont.aspx.

6. Josh Katz, "'Duck Dynasty' vs. 'Modern Family': 50 Maps of the U.S. Cultural Divide," *New York Times*, December 27, 2016.

7. For a more comprehensive discussion of the ratings gaps between the

NFL and other major American sports leagues, see my October 10, 2017, *National Review* essay, "Can the NFL Survive National Polarization?"

8. FiveThirtyEight's "Polarization" tag can be found here: https://fivethirtyeight.com/tag/polarization.

Chapter 2: Geography Plus Culture Plus Fear Equals Secession

1. You can read the entire Cornerstone speech here: http://teachingamericanhistory.org/library/document/cornerstone-speech.

2. I describe Nat Turner's actions more fully in my *National Review* essay, "Honor Resistance to Slavery, but Don't Honor Nat Turner," October 22, 2016.

3. For an excellent, detailed description of Turner's rebellion and the resulting white backlash, read Mark St. John Erickson, "Remembering the Horror of Nat Turner's Rebellion on This Day in 1831," *Daily Press*, August 21, 2018.

4. Ibid.

5. Ta-Nehisi Coates, "Was Nat Turner Right?," *The Atlantic*, October 1, 2012.

6. James McPherson, *Battle Cry of Freedom: The Civil War Era* (New York: Oxford University Press, 1988), 209.

7. Ibid., 209–210.

8. Ibid., 210–211.

9. You can read Georgia's complete Declaration of Secession here: http://www.civildiscourse-historyblog.com/blog/2018/7/1/secession-documents-georgia.

10. You can read Mississippi's "Declaration of the Immediate Causes Which Induce and Justify the Secession of the State of Mississippi from the Federal Union" here: http://avalon.law.yale.edu/19th_century/csa_missec.asp.

11. You can read South Carolina's "Declaration of the Immediate Causes Which Induce and Justify the Secession of the State of South Carolina from the Federal Union" here: https://avalon.law.yale.edu/19th_century/csa_scarsec.asp.

12. You can read Texas's "Declaration of the Causes Which Impel the State of Texas to Secede from the Federal Union" here: https://www.tsl.texas.gov/ref/abouttx/secession/2feb1861.html.

Chapter 3: The Kindling Awaits the Spark of Fear

1. David Bernstein, "The Supreme Court Oral Argument That Cost the Democrats the Presidency," *Washington Post*, December 7, 2016.

2. You can read a complete copy of the Trump administration's lawsuit here: https://www.nytimes.com/interactive/2018/03/06/us/politics/document -justice-lawsuit-california.html.

Chapter 4: America Cannot Repeat Even Its Recent History of Violence

1. Bobby Allyn, "1969: A Year of Bombings," *New York Times*, August 27, 2009.

2. "1967 Detroit Riots," History.com, September 27, 2017.

3. You can read the entire Kerner Commission Report here: https:// haasinstitute.berkeley.edu/1968-kerner-report.

Chapter 5: How an Academic Paper Explains America

1. You can read Sunstein's original paper at this link: https://chicagoun bound.uchicago.edu/cgi/viewcontent.cgi?article=1541&context=law_and _economics.

2. Jocelyn Kelly, "In Polarized Era, Fewer Americans Hold a Mix of Conservative and Liberal Views," Pew Research Center, October 23, 2017.

Chapter 6: Churches and Cities, the Core of Group Polarization

1. Gregory Smith and Jessica Martinez, "How the Faithful Voted: A Preliminary 2016 Analysis," Pew Research Center, November 9, 2016.

2. You can read the resolution at the following link: http://www.sbc.net /resolutions/773/resolution-on-moral-character-of-public-officials.

3. "Backing Trump, White Evangelicals Flip Flop on Importance of Candidate Character," PRRI/Brookings Survey, October 19, 2016, https:// www.prri.org/research/prri-brookings-oct-19-poll-politics-election -clinton-double-digit-lead-trump.

4. https://sfelections.org/results/20161108.

5. https://abc7ny.com/politics/how-each-nyc-borough-voted-(hint-clinton-di dnt-win-them-all)/1598306.

6. Ibid.

7. https://www.nytimes.com/elections/2016/results/district-of-columbia.

8. Ibid.

9. This section of the book is adapted from my *National Review* essay, "The Democrats' God Gap," May 2, 2018.

10. "When Americans Say They Believe in God, What Do They Mean?," Pew Research Center, April 25, 2018.

11. Emma Green, "Politics as the New Religion for Progressive Democrats," *The Atlantic*, October 11, 2018.

Chapter 7: Politics Trumps Everything

1. Patrick Egan, "Identity as Dependent Variable: How Americans Shift Their Identities to Better Align with Their Politics," Wilf Family Department of Politics, New York University, September 10, 2018, https://rubenson.org/wp-content/uploads/2018/09/egan-tpbw18.pdf.

2. Ibid.

3. Perry Bacon Jr., "Democrats Are Wrong About Republicans. Republicans Are Wrong About Democrats," FiveThirtyEight, June 26, 2018.

4. Ibid.

5. Ibid.

6. Ben Sasse, "Politics Can't Solve Our Political Problems," *Wall Street Journal*, October 12, 2018.

Chapter 8: From Extreme to Mainstream, Time and Again

1. The evolution of laws on the right to carry is outlined in Charles C. W. Cooke's *National Review* essay, "Charlie Sykes Is Wrong to Call Constitutional Carry Nuts," October 8, 2017. In that essay he shared a chart by Jeff Dege detailing the year-by-year change in state right-to-carry laws.

Chapter 9: The Shifting Window of Acceptable Discourse

1. This section of the book is adapted in part from my *National Review* essay, "For Good and Ill, Donald Trump Has Brought Discussion of Political Impossibilities into the Open," December 8, 2015.

2. To review the Mackinac Center resource page on the origin and meaning of the term "Overton window," please see https://www.mackinac.org/overtonwindow.

3. Ibid.

4. The discussion of the fraught nature of the gun debate is adapted from my *National Review* essay "The Gun-Control Debate Could Break America," February 22, 2018.

5. The video is embedded in this tweet: https://twitter.com/NRATV/status/966534627522301952.

6. Kevin Williamson, "Another Misfire at the *New York Times*," *National Review*, February 21, 2018.

Chapter 10: Losing the Free Speech Culture

1. Greg Lukianoff and Jonathan Haidt, "The Coddling of the American Mind," *The Atlantic*, September 2015.

2. Stanley Kurtz, "Year of the Shout-Down: It Was Worse Than You Think," *National Review*, May 31, 2017.

3. Mark Gomez, "Nine People Arrested at Ben Shapiro Event at UC-Berkeley," *Mercury News*, September 15, 2017.

4. You can read the entire McLaughlin and Associates survey here: http://c8 .nrostatic.com/sites/default/files/NATL%20Undergrad%209-27-17%20 Presentation%20(1).pdf.

5. John Villasenor, "Views Among College Students Regarding the First Amendment: Results from a New Survey," Brookings Institution, September 18, 2017.

6. You can read the entire Gallup and Knight Survey here: https:// kf-site-production.s3.amazonaws.com/publications/pdfs/000/000/248 /original/Knight_Foundation_Free_Expression_on_Campus_2017.pdf.

7. You can read Frederick Douglass's "Plea for Free Speech in Boston" here: https://frederickdouglass.infoset.io/islandora/object/islandora:2129# page/1/mode/1up.

Chapter 11: Losing a Common Political Language

1. I detailed and linked to Jeong's tweets and the tweets in response in my *National Review* essay "Yes, Anti-White Racism Exists," August 2, 2018.

2. Ezinine Ukoha, "Why the Notion of 'Anti-White Racism' Is a Purposed Lie," *Medium*, August 6, 2018.

Chapter 15: Pluralism, a Beginner's Guide

1. Peter Leyden and Ruy Teixeira, "The Great Lesson of California in America's New Civil War," *Medium*, January 19, 2018.

2. Ibid.

Chapter 16: Rediscover Tolerance

1. This section of the book is adapted from my essay "Let's Talk About Tolerance," published on April 6, 2018, in *National Review*.

2. Scott Alexander, "I Can Tolerate Anything Except the Outgroup," Slate Star Codex, September 30, 2014, available at https://slatestarcodex.com /2014/09/30/i-can-tolerate-anything-except-the-outgroup.

3. To take one example, on August 16, 2017, a number of progressives

(including CNN host Christopher Cuomo) retweeted a meme showing American soldiers storming the beaches at Normandy under the caption "Anti-Fascists Disrupting a Large Gathering of White Supremacists," https://twitter.com/chriscuomo/status/897820041273626626?lang=en.

4. Robert Shibley, "Free Speech Lawsuits Filed Against Penn State and Temple," Foundation for Individual Rights in Education, February 23, 2006.

5. "6 Tales of Censorship in the Golden Age of Free Speech," *Wired*, January 16, 2018.

6. Gabby Galvin, "Study: Middle School Is Key to Girls' Coding Interest," *U.S. News and World Report*, October 20, 2016.

7. You can read Damore's complaint at https://www.dropbox.com/s /f6p02fijxrd7c6m/20180108%20Damore%20-%20Complaint_fs.pdf?dl=0.

8. You can read the Masterpiece Cakeshop ruling here: https://www .supremecourt.gov/opinions/17pdf/16-111_j4el.pdf.

9. The relevant allegations against Scardina and the Colorado Civil Rights Commission can be read here: http://www.adfmedia.org/files /MasterpieceCakeshopComplaint.pdf.

Chapter 17: Can Anyone Pass the Tolerance Test?

1. This section of the book is adapted from my essay "This Culture War Isn't About the Flag; It's About Conscience," published on September 27, 2017, in *National Review*.

2. You can read the entire Supreme Court opinion in *West Virginia State Board of Education v. Barnette* here: https://www.law.cornell.edu /supremecourt/text/319/624#ZO-319_US_624n1.

3. Eugene Scott, "President Trump Says NFL Players Who Protest Shouldn't Be in the Game—and Maybe Not in the Country," *Washington Post*, May 24, 2018.

4. Alex Lardieri, "Trump to Hannity, You Can't Disrespect Our Flag," *U.S. News and World Report*, October 12, 2017.

Chapter 18: Can Moments of Grace Make a Movement of Grace?

1. This section of the book is adapted from my essay "The Dan Crenshaw Moment," published November 12, 2018, in *National Review*.

2. You can watch the *Saturday Night Live* segment here: https://www .youtube.com/watch?time_continue=2&v=GKaakjMVtyE.

3. Dan Zak, "Dan Crenshaw Started the Week as a Punchline and Ended

It as a Star. The Real Story Came Before That," *Washington Post*, November 11, 2018.

4. Lisa Respers France, "Ellen DeGeneres Explains Hanging Out with Her Friend George W. Bush," CNN, October 8, 2019.

5. Molly Roberts, "Ellen DeGeneres Tells America She's Better Than Us," *Washington Post*, October 11, 2019.

6. You can see the full study at https://perceptiongap.us.

7. Kevin Drum, "Nutpicking," *Washington Monthly*, August 11, 2006.

Chapter 20: Immigration Breaks the Federalist Will

1. You can read the full text of A.B. 103 here: https://leginfo.legislature.ca.gov/faces/billTextClient.xhtml?bill_id=201720180AB103.

2. You can read the full text of the California Values Act here: https://leginfo.legislature.ca.gov/faces/billTextClient.xhtml?bill_id=201720180SB54.

3. You can read the text of the Immigrant Worker Protection Act here: https://leginfo.legislature.ca.gov/faces/billNavClient.xhtml?bill_id=201720180AB450.

4. The description of the text and purpose of the Arizona law is taken from *Arizona et al. v. United States*, 567 U.S. 387 (2012). You can read the text here: https://www.supremecourt.gov/opinions/11pdf/11-182.pdf.

5. In a July 2018 ruling, a federal district court judge dismissed part of the Trump administration's suit against California and put part of the law on hold. As of the time of writing, the case is still pending. You can read the trial court's preliminary ruling here: https://www.documentcloud.org/documents/4576513-7-5-18-US-v-California-Opinion-PI.html.

Chapter 21: Could California Health Care Reform Revive American Federalism?

1. You can read the text of the act here: https://leginfo.legislature.ca.gov/faces/billNavClient.xhtml?bill_id=201720180SB562.

2. Sally Pipes, "Is Statewide Single-Payer Feasible, or Is It Just California Dreamin'?," *Forbes*, June 25, 2018.

3. See https://leginfo.legislature.ca.gov/faces/billHistoryClient.xhtml?bill_id=201720180SB562.

4. For an excellent description of the mechanics of California single-payer, read Patricia Cohen and Reed Abelson, "Single-Payer Healthcare in California: Here's What It Would Take," *New York Times*, May 25, 2018.

Chapter 22: Federalism Ends Where the Bill of Rights Begins

1. You can read the full text of the "straw law" here: https://leginfo.legislature
   .ca.gov/faces/billTextClient.xhtml?bill_id=201720180AB1884.

2. Christian Britschgi, "California Considers $1,000 Fine for Waiters Of-
   fering Unsolicited Plastic Straws," *Reason*, January 25, 2018.

3. John Bowden, "California Has Sued the Trump Administration 46 Times.
   Here Are the Lawsuits," *The Hill*, January 20, 2019.

4. For a description of the constitutional problems with California's high-
   capacity magazine restrictions, see this July 2018 Ninth Circuit Court
   decision blocking implementation of the law: http://michellawyers
   .com/wp-content/uploads/2018/07/Duncan-2018-07-17-Memorandum
   -Affirming.pdf.

5. National Institute of Family and Life Advocates v. Becerra, 138 S.Ct.
   2361 (2018).

6. "Health Insurance Coverage: Early Release of Estimates from the National Health Interview Survey, 2006, Centers for Disease Control,"
   June 2007, located at https://www.cdc.gov/nchs/data/nhis/earlyrelease
   /insur200706.pdf.

7. You can read the full text of the bill here: https://www.congress.gov/bill
   /116th-congress/senate-bill/1914.

Conclusion: A Call for Courage

1. Adapted from my essay "The Drive to Become 'Fox News Famous' Hurts
   the Right," *National Review*, August 30, 2016.

2. Adapted from my "The Patriotism of Deeds," *National Review*, May 28,
   2018.

INDEX

abolitionism movement, 45–48.
    See also slavery
abortion
    and Calexit scenario, 142
    and Clinton administration, 95
    pro-life movement, 3, 13, 52, 71,
        146–147, 149, 231, 250
    Roe v. Wade, 14, 31, 144–145, 151
    state legislation and laws, 31–32,
        231
    and Texit scenario, 144–146,
        149–151, 153, 162
    and tolerance, 110
Adams, John, 244, 251–252, 255
Ahmari, Sohrab, 24
al Qaeda, 6, 7, 8
Alexander, Scott (pseudonym),
    185–186
Alito, Samuel, 51
alt-right, 11, 103, 243
American Civil War
    "Cornerstone" speech (Stephens), 40
    declarations of secession, 40–41, 47
    Lost Cause myth, 40
    reasons for southern secession, 40–48
    and religious sects, 19
    and revivals, 163
    surrender at Appomattox Court
        House, 40
    Virginia's role in, 37, 44–45
antifa, 57–58, 187
anti-Semitism, 11, 57
Anton, Michael, 10
Asch, Solomon, 65–66
Atkins, Toni, 223–224

Bacon, Perry, Jr., 82–83
Beauchamp, Zack, 111–112
Bernstein, David, 51

Bible
    Book of Acts, 249
    "God gap," 79
    King David, 73–74
    on marriage, 51
    Micah, 208–209
    Proverbs 15:22, 64
"big sort," 34, 69, 89, 180, 213
Bill of Rights
    and Civil War amendments, 215
    and Ending Support for Internet
        Censorship Act, 238–239
    and federalism, 210, 227–228,
        231–240
    First Amendment, 19–21, 52,
        106–108, 187, 231–232, 238
    and health care, 234–236
    and Madison, James, 19, 22
    and national conservatism, 237–238
    purpose of, 90
    Second Amendment, 37, 65, 88, 97,
        122, 124, 127, 131–132, 231, 242
    and tolerance, 90, 210
    See also free speech
Birth of a Nation, The (2016), 44
Bishop, Bill, 34. *See also* "big sort"
Breitbart (website), 103
Breitbart, Andrew, 94
Breyer, Stephen, 220
Brown, Jerry, 230, 231
Brown, John, 45–47, 137
Bush, George H. W., 3, 60–61
Bush, George W., 5, 9, 72, 160, 205

Calexit (hypothetical scenario)
    abolishment of filibuster, 141
    congressional response to crisis,
        136–137
    court challenge to legislation, 122–123

Calexit (*continued*)
    fear of minority rule, 177
    geographic separation, 121
    gubernatorial call for secession,
        139–141
    gun confiscation, 127–128, 134, 138
    inciting incident (school shooting),
        119–120
    initial presidential response to
        crisis, 123–125
    international impact of, 165–174
    intolerance, 139
    legislative response to shooting,
        120–122
    polarization, 121, 137, 143
    Posse Comitatus Act, 137
    presidential political and strategic
        response to secession, 141–143
    protests and federal response,
        125–126
    response to Supreme Court decision,
        133–137
    sanctuary siege, 125–126
    Supreme Court arguments and
        decision, 128–133
    "Trinity Ambush," 137–139
    vote for secession, 142–143
California
    and Bill of Rights, 229–234,
        236–237, 240
    Children's Health Insurance Pro-
        gram (CHIP), 224
    economy of, 35
    First Amendment legislation,
        231–232
    lawsuits against Trump administra-
        tion, 230
    plastic straw law, 229–230, 233
    response to U.S. withdrawal from
        Paris climate accords, 231
    sanctuary movement, 53–54,
        125–127, 132, 218, 230, 232
    Second Amendment legislation,
        231–232
    See also Calexit (hypothetical scenario)
Carney, Timothy, 23
cascade effects, 67–69, 71–75, 79
    definition of, 67–68
    King David cascade, 73–74
    secular social justice cascade, 75

Charlottesville rally and protest
    (2017), 13, 113
China, 15, 53, 166, 168–173
church attendance, 34, 36, 84, 162–163
Civil Rights Act (1964), 41
civil rights law, 41, 87, 150, 192
civil rights movement, 62, 108
Civil Rights Renewal Act, 150
Clinton, Bill
    foreign and domestic policies of, 95
    impeachment of, 72
    and Overton window, 95–96
    and scandal, 4
Clinton, Hillary, 10, 37, 72, 76, 87
clustering, 2, 33, 37, 78, 99–100
Cold War, 5, 212, 245
coronavirus, 62, 84
Cruz, Ted, 213
cultural appropriation, 76

Damore, James, 188–194
Declaration of Independence, 22, 227
Douglass, Frederick, 27, 107, 245
Drum, Kevin, 207

Egan, Patrick, 81–82, 83
elections
    landslide counties, 1, 32, 69
    landslide elections, 60–61, 148,
        178–179
    midterm election of 2010, 178–179
    midterm election of 2014, 179
    midterm election of 2018, 32–33,
        179, 233
    presidential election of 1972, 60
    presidential election of 1980, 60
    presidential election of 1984, 60
    presidential election of 1988, 35,
        60–61
    presidential election of 1992, 32
    presidential election of 2008, 72,
        178, 235
    presidential election of 2012, 72, 179
    presidential election of 2016, 10,
        32, 51, 69, 71–73, 76, 79, 179,
        223, 248
Electoral College, 13
    and Calexit scenario, 142, 177
    presidential election of 1972, 60
    presidential election of 1980, 60

presidential election of 1984, 60
presidential election of 1988, 35,
  60–61
Emerson, Ralph Waldo, 45
Evangelical Christianity
  diversity of, 75
  and election of 2004, 72
  and election of 2008, 72
  and election of 2012, 72
  and election of 2016, 71, 72, 73, 76
  elites and progressives on, 51–52, 75
  and Jackson, Andrew, 147
  and King David cascade, 73–74
  and partisanship, 72
  and Republican Party, 71–72, 82

Facebook, 96, 238–239
Fauntroy, Walter, 108
federalism
  and Bill of Rights, 229–240
  and Constitution, 182
  diminished belief in, 210–211
  failures of, 211–212
  and Founders, 220–221, 227–228,
    236–237
  and Fourteenth Amendment, 132
  and health care, 223–228
  and immigration, 54, 217–222
  protection of, 19
  rediscovering, 214–216, 241
  and sanctuary laws, 54
  and state laws, 54
  and tolerance, 210
Federalist No. 10, 17–19, 25, 27,
  179–180
financial crisis of 2007–2008, 8
FiveThirtyEight (website), 39,
  82–83
Foundation for Individual Rights in
  Education (FIRE), 101
Founders, 17, 22, 89–90, 173
  and diversity of founding, 20–21
  and federalism, 220–221, 227–228,
    236–237
Framers, 131, 228
free speech
  and antebellum South, 107–108
  and censorship, 101–102, 104–107,
    110, 116, 157, 197–199
  and civil rights era, 108

First Amendment, 19–21, 52,
  106–108, 187, 231–232, 238
  and Gitlow v. New York, 107–108
  and hate speech, 104–106
  and higher education, 101–109, 187,
    200
  and political correctness, 55, 102,
    255
  public opinion on, 104–107
Friends, 76, 77

Game of Thrones, 37
Garland, Merrick, 13
geography, 33–39
  and American division, 31–39
  and Calexit scenario, 121
  and civil rights era, 60
  and Civil War, 56–60
  contiguous red and blue enclaves,
    25, 49, 56, 60, 234, 236
  and coronavirus recession, 62
  and culture, 25, 40–48, 49, 54–55
  and group polarization, 89
  and gun laws, 55
  and immigration laws, 54–55
  mobility and economic prosperity,
    84–85
  and Reagan era, 60–61
  red and blue walls, 33–36, 50–55
  and secularization, 78
  sorting and separation, 1, 2, 9–10,
    89, 116, 121, 178, 213
  and sports, 37–38
  and television, 37
  and twenty-first century, 9–10,
    61–62
  and voting habits, 1
Gingrich, Newt, 4
Ginsburg, Ruth Bader, 220
Goldberg, Jonah, 23, 249
Google, 188–194
grace, moments of, 202–209
  Crenshaw-Davidson incident,
    202–205
  DeGeneres-Bush incident, 205–206
  and media, 207–208
  and partisanship, 206–208
Greeley, Horace, 46
Green, Emma, 80
group bias, 65

group polarization
    and Calexit scenario, 121, 137, 143
    and cities, 75–77
    and gun control debate, 87–91, 121
    "The Law of Group Polarization"
        (Sunstein), 63–69, 71, 72, 73–74,
        75, 79–80, 86, 89
    and LGBT rights movement, 77–78,
        88, 89, 91
    power and impact of, 81–85, 86
    and religion, 71–75
    and secularization, 77–80
    See also negative polarization;
        polarization
gun control, 65, 91, 99
    and Calexit scenario, 119–120, 122,
        124, 138
    gun culture, 87, 99
    gun ownership, 36, 120–123,
        127–128, 130, 134, 137
    National Rifle Association (NRA),
        97–98, 127
    and Texit scenario, 149–150
    See also mass shootings; school
        shootings
gun legislation and laws
    concealed-carry states, 120
    constitutional carry states, 88, 89
    "may issue" states, 88
    "no issue" states, 88
    "shall issue" states, 88, 120

Haidt, Jonathan, 102, 104
Hamilton (musical), 208–209
Hamilton, Alexander, 244
Hannity, Sean, 198–199, 200
Harpers Ferry, raid on, 45–47, 137
hate speech, 56, 104–106
Hawley, Josh, 238–239
health care
    Affordable Care Act (Obamacare),
        234–236
    and Bill of Rights, 230–236
    and Clinton, Bill, 95
    and conservative/progressive split,
        250, 255
    Healthy California Act, 223–228,
        230
    in Massachusetts (Romneycare),
        234–236

Medicaid, 136, 212, 224, 226
Medicare, 136, 212, 223, 224, 226,
    227
Medicare for All, 223, 224
    political rhetoric of, 56
    single-payer, 146, 150, 222, 223
    universal, 145
higher education
    and culture, 51–52, 248–249
    and free speech, 101–109, 187,
        200
    and gender, 188–190
    and Title IX, 102, 242
    and violence, 103–104
Howells, William Dean, 46

immigration
    Arizona v. United States, 218–221
    and federalism, 54, 217–222
    and geography, 54–55
    Support Our Law Enforcement and
        Safe Neighborhoods Act (Arizona),
        218–221
    See also sanctuary laws
Iraq War, 5–9, 11, 12, 183, 256
Islam, 7, 34

Jefferson, Thomas, 22, 244, 254
Jenner, Caitlyn, 92
Jeong, Sarah, 111–115
Jim Crow laws, 41, 55, 108, 145, 211,
    214, 232, 245
Joachim, David, 112
Judge, Mike, 78

Kaepernick, Colin, 38
Kennedy, Anthony, 219–220
Kennedy, John F., 59
Kennedy, Robert, 59
Kerry, John, 72
King, Martin Luther, Jr., 59
Kipnis, Laura, 102
Kors, Alan Charles, 101
Kurtz, Stanley, 103

Lara, Ricardo, 223–224
Leyden, Peter, 178
LGBT legislation and court cases
    Defense of Marriage Act (DOMA),
        94–96

Masterpiece Cakeshop v. Colorado Civil Rights Commission, 194–195, 200
Obergefell v. Hodges, 50–51, 94
LGBT rights and issues
    and California, 231
    and Christianity, 77
    and geographic divisions, 55
    and gun rights movement, 88, 89
    and identity, 82
    same-sex marriage, 50–51, 87, 88, 94, 194–195, 200, 205
    transgender population, 87, 92, 186, 195
liberalism
    and cultural decline, 24
    definition of, 23
    and Founding, 89–90
    and moderation, 252
    and pluralism, 181, 182
    and tolerance, 27, 184, 186–187
likability gap, 69
Lincoln, Abraham, 43, 48, 244–245
Loesch, Dana, 97, 98
Lukianoff, Greg, 101–102, 104, 109

Mackinac Center for Public Policy, 93
Maddow, Rachel, 200
Madison, James
    and Bill of Rights, 19
    Federalist No. 10, 17–19, 25, 27, 179–180
    leadership of, 244
    on pluralism, 19, 22, 25–26
majority rule, 177
Martin, George R. R., 37
Mason, Lilliana, 82–83
mass shootings, 13, 57. *See also* school shootings
McPherson, James, 45–46
#MeToo movement, 248
microaggression, 76
Midwest (United States), 124
    and abortion, 144–145, 149, 151
    Upper Midwest, 33, 35–36
minority rule, 177
moderation, political, 115, 214, 239, 252
Morey, Daryl, 53
Murray, Charles, 23, 103

NATO, 166–168
negative polarization
    and Calexit scenario, 137
    challenge of, 90–92, 137, 241, 244, 251–252
    definition of, 2
    and ideological polarization, 69–70, 237
    and the military, 160
    and Overton window, 96–97
    and political virtue, 251–252
    and Texit scenario, 160, 164
    and tolerance, 185, 200
    See also group polarization; polarization
New England, 33, 135, 143. *See also* Northeast (United States)
New South, 5, 147, 162
Newsom, Gavin, 225
9/11, 9, 10, 203
Nixon, Richard, 60
Northeast (United States), 35, 36, 37. *See also* New England
Norton, Charles Eliot, 45
Norton, Quinn, 110–111
nuclear weapons (hypothetical scenarios), 141, 143, 160, 168–173

Obama, Barack
    Affordable Care Act, 234–236
    and birtherism, 8–9
    and Evangelical vote, 72
    and gender-identity directives, 77–78
    "God and guns" comment, 36
    lawsuit against Arizona immigration law, 219, 221
Obergefell v. Hodges, 50–51, 94
Olasky, Marvin, 221
Old South, 11, 43, 162
Orwell, George, 97
Overton, Joseph, 93
Overton window, 93–97, 99–100, 107, 110, 112

Pacific air and naval conflict (hypothetical scenario), 169–173
Pacific Coast states, 33, 35, 125, 135. *See also* California
Parker, Nate, 44

Parker, Theodore, 45
patriotism, 38, 196–197, 253–256
Pax Americana, 165
Pelosi, Nancy, 213
Phillips, Jack, 194–195
Pipes, Sally, 224
pluralism, 177–184
    and defense of rights of others, 181
    and defense of rights of self-
        governance, 181
    definition of healthy pluralism, 23
    impact of hatred and intolerance on,
        182–183
    Madison, James on, 19, 22, 25–26
    and partisanship, 24–25, 90,
        237–238
    and right of voluntary association,
        20, 181
    and surrender, 27–28, 180–181
    and tolerance, 241
polarization, 9–10
    and federalism, 214, 221–222,
        236–237, 250
    history of, 23, 60, 61
    and justice, 256
    and moral courage, 253
    and pluralism, 177, 178, 180
    See also group polarization; negative
        polarization
police power, 227
political correctness, 55, 102, 255
Posse Comitatus Act, 133–134, 137
predeliberation bias, 64–66, 71,
    75–76
Presbyterian church, 71, 74
pro-life movement, 3, 13, 52, 71,
    146–147, 149, 231, 250
protests over police violence, 15
Putnam, Robert, 23

racism, 110–115, 190–191
    anti-white, 112–115
    definitions of, 110–113
    and hate speech, 105
    racist slurs, 112, 238
    and Trump, Donald, 12–13
    and violence, 113–114
Reagan, Ronald, 3, 60–61
Religious Freedom Restoration Act
    (federal law), 95–96

Religious Freedom Restoration Act
    (Indiana), 52
religious liberty, 71
    and Clinton, Bill, 75
    legislation, 52, 55, 77, 95–96
    and pluralism, 181
    and polarization, 87
    and Texit scenario, 142, 146, 149
Republican Governors Association, 149
Roberts, John, 220
Roberts, Molly, 205–206
Roe v. Wade, 14, 31, 144–145, 151
Roosevelt, Franklin D., 212, 245
Rubio, Marco, 97, 98

safetyism, 104
sanctuary laws
    Calexit scenario, 125–127, 132
    and federalism, 218, 230, 232
    sanctuary cities, 53–54, 232
    sanctuary states, 218, 230, 232
Sanders, Bernie, 223, 224
Sasse, Ben, 83–85
Scalia, Antonin, 220–221
Scalise, Steve (baseball field shooting),
    15, 57
Scardina, Autumn, 195
school shootings
    and Calexit scenario, 119–129
    Columbine shooting (1999), 119
    Parkland shooting (2018), 97–99
secularism
    and blue wall, 36
    and Evangelicals, 73
    and identity, 34
    and race, 5
    secularization, 1–2 77–78
    and social justice cascade, 75, 77–80
    and "Texit," 146, 162, 164
September 11, 2001, terrorist attacks,
    9, 10, 203
Sex and the City, 76
Shapiro, Ben, 11, 103, 104
Shays's Rebellion, 126
Sherman, William Tecumseh, 6, 245
Silicon Valley
    and Calexit scenario, 149, 157–159
    and diversity, 188
    and free speech, 106
    and tolerance, 188–194

Silicon Valley, 78
Silverglate, Harvey, 101
slavery
    abolitionism movement, 45–48
    and Founders, 22
    history of (United States), 41–42
    raid on Harpers Ferry, 45–47, 137
    See also American Civil War
social media
    and Calexit scenario, 122–123, 127,
        138
    and Ending Support for Internet
        Censorship Act, 238–239
    Facebook, 96, 238–239
    and ideology, 15, 96, 193–194, 229
    Instagram, 238
    and Texit scenario, 157, 158
    trolling, 11, 111
    and violence, 57–58
    See also Twitter
Sotomayor, Sonia, 220
South (United States)
    antebellum era, 42–43, 45–48
    Civil War, 60, 211
    and division, 35 (*See also* Texit
        [hypothetical scenario])
    military bases, 160–161
    New South, 5, 147, 162
    Old South, 11, 43, 162
    state abortion legislation, 144
Southeast (United States), 33, 35, 124
Southeastern Conference (NCAA),
    33, 35
Southern Baptist church, 72–73, 146
Southern Baptist Convention, 72–73
sports
    college football, 33, 38
    and gender-identity directives,
        77–78
    and geography, 37–38
    national anthem protests, 38,
        198–199
    NBA, 37–38, 53
    NFL, 38, 195, 198–200
    and Title IX, 87
states' rights, 40, 211
Stephens, Alexander, 40
Stowe, Harriet Beecher, 245
Sunstein, Cass, 63–69, 71, 72, 73–74,
    75, 79–80, 86, 89

Tapper, Jake, 97
Tea Party movement, 178–179
Teixeira, Ruy, 178
Texit (hypothetical scenario)
    abolishment of filibuster, 145–146,
        149
    and abortion, 144–146, 149–151,
        153, 162
    Columbus Conference (meeting of
        president and Texas governor),
        161–163
    congressional response to crisis,
        157–158
    corporate boycotts, 156–157, 159
    Court-packing, 145–146, 150, 151,
        154
    death of governor of Alabama,
        153–154
    economic boycotts, 164
    election of governor, 144, 149
    fear of majority rule, 177
    great migration, 164
    gubernatorial and state legislative
        response to boycotts, 158–159
    international impact of, 165–174
    internet blackout, 157–159
    intolerance, 146, 149
    Lexington Declaration, 149–150,
        151, 154–155
    military partisanship, 159–161
    neo-Confederates, 158, 162
    overturning of *Roe v. Wade,*
        144–145, 151
    polarization, 160, 164
    presidential demands of loyalty, 157
    presidential election, 148–149
    presidential response to states'
        legislation, 155–156
    resolution of and vote for secession,
        163–164
    state guards' rebellion against
        federal government, 156
    violence, 158
    voter boycott, 163
Thirteenth Amendment, 41
Thoreau, Henry David, 46
Tocqueville, Alexis de, 21–22, 23
tolerance, 185–195
    and corporate culture, 187–188
    definition of, 185–186

tolerance (*continued*)
 and partisanship, 185–188, 190,
  193–195
 and polarization, 196–201
 and Silicon Valley, 188–194
 and *West Virginia v. Barnette*,
  196–198, 199
trifecta states, 33
trigger warnings, 76
Trump, Donald
 Access Hollywood tape, 12
 and birtherism, 9
 border wall, 230
 California's lawsuits against Trump
  administration, 230
 on Crenshaw, Dan, 204
 and Evangelicals, 71–72, 74–76
 "The Flight 93 Election" (Anton),
  10, 250
 impeachment of, 15–16
 and King David Cascade, 73–74
 and lawsuit against California's
  immigration laws, 53–54, 221
 Muslim travel ban, 12
 and national anthem protests, 38,
  198–199
 and nationalism, 253
 online treatment of critics of, 11,
  243–244
 and patriotism, 253
 presidential election of 2016, 10, 32,
  51, 69, 71–73, 76, 79, 179, 223, 248
 and Putin, Vladimir, 12
 rallies, 58
 and sanctuary cities, 53–54
 withdrawal from Paris climate
  accords, 231
Tubman, Harriet, 245
Turner, Nat, 44, 47
Twitter
 Crenshaw-Davidson incident,
  204–206
 and Ending Support for Internet
  Censorship Act, 238, 239
 harassment on, 11, 61

 and ideology, 96, 111–112, 114, 200
 and nutpicking, 207–208
 political Twitter, 56, 100, 110–112,
  114, 200, 205
 See also social media

Upper Midwest (United States), 33,
 35–36

Verrilli, Donald B., Jr., 51, 52
Vietnam War, 58, 61–62, 245
violence, 56–62
 civil rights era, 58–59
 and communication technology,
  57–58
 and fear, 56–57
 Kent State shooting, 58
 Kerner Commission Report on, 59
 mass shootings, 13, 57
 school shootings, 97–99, 119–129

Walking Dead, The, 37
wall, border, 230
wall, geographic and political, 33–36,
 50–55
 blue wall, 35–36, 54–55
 red wall, 35, 36, 50, 52–53, 55
Warren, Elizabeth, 224
Washington, George, 208, 244
West (United States)
 economy of, 35
 "red West," 123, 127
 West Coast, 33, 35, 125, 135
 See also Calexit (hypothetical scenario); California
West Virginia v. Barnette, 196–198,
 199
Western alliance, 165–167
white nationalism, 11, 57
white supremacy, 11, 13, 57, 211
Williamson, Kevin, 99, 110, 214
World War I, 172
World War II, 169, 197, 212, 245

Yiannopoulos, Milo, 103

Nancy French

DAVID FRENCH is a senior editor at *The Dispatch,* a columnist for *Time,* and the author or coauthor of several books, most recently *Rise of ISIS: A Threat We Can't Ignore,* a *New York Times* bestseller. He lives in Tennessee.